I was raised in a denomination that
full-time international missionaries. I
learned how many churches and par
their own support. While recognizing
identifies its growing number of weaknesses, along with the advantages, especially
for Majority World missionaries, to adopt other models that may even be more
biblical. Canvassing an encouraging variety of these, Welch makes a persuasive
case for us to vary our models when possible, to best meet today's needs. Highly
recommended.

CRAIG L. BLOMBERG, PhD
Distinguished Professor Emeritus, New Testament, Denver Seminary

Tim Welch challenges us in this important research to reconsider how we fund
missions in today's context in which we are sending workers from everywhere to
everywhere. Our mindset needs to be challenged and reframed—through biblical
reflection, global statistics, and with contextual relevance we are given a wide
variety of models to grow mission funding. There is no "one size fits all," Tim
presents an A-Z of case studies/models that moves away from the more traditional
Western context to diversified models. The stakes are high, creativity is essential,
and the Gospel call remains central as we step out in faith with Jehovah Jireh to see
the nations reached.

EMMA BREWSTER
SIM Global Director of Ministry Outreach, South Africa

Tim Welch has written a well-documented approach to the vital issue of funding
global mission. He understands the issues related to this subject through his own
mission journey serving SIM for thirty-one years in Cote d'Ivoire. This book
is a must-read for mission donors, foundations, prospective missionaries, and
mission leaders.

LUIS BUSH
President, Transform World Connections
Former CEO, Partners International
Former International Director, COMIBAM & AD2000 and Beyond Movement

I highly recommend this game-changing work by Tim Welch. Financing outreach
among the least reached peoples through the impassioned Majority World Church
is one of the greatest challenges facing contemporary mission practitioners. Welch
both encourages and challenges mission practitioners to tear down outdated "faith-
based" support structures in favor of more innovative approaches. He introduces
culturally relevant funding models; the effective adoption of the models presented
in this work will allow the Majority World church to expand even farther into
restricted access countries where the gospel is most needed. I recommend this
book to anyone serious about adaptive change in mission funding, but especially
to those who labor daily to fulfill God's mission in the world by walking alongside
our brothers in the Majority World church.

LLOYD S. CHINN
Global Director, World Venture, Africa

New Funding Models for Global Mission is an innovative book that will be a useful resource for those in the ministry. Learning strategic funding will help us move forward with our ministries.

DAMPLES DULCERO-BACLAGON
Managing Editor, Asian Missions Advance

New Funding Models for Global Mission by Tim Welch is an eclectic assemblage of mission support models. As an "African missionary" in a pioneering leadership role within an indigenous mission agency, I can strongly relate with every aspect of the contents of this book. Tim highlights and articulates various Biblical and practicable examples and models of mission support and involvement. I strongly recommend this book especially to the churches, mission agencies, missionaries, and mission mobilizers from the Majority World, which are perceived as constituting the largest mission forces, now and in the future.

REUBEN EZEMADU
International Director, Christian Missionary Foundation
Continental Coordinator, Movement For African National Initiatives
Ibadan, Nigeria

As the Christian mission now occurs from everywhere to everywhere, mission personnel, strategies, models, and funding are going to be more diversified than ever before. Tim Welch explores many emerging realities of the Global South regions and provides Biblical reflections on the mission task and resources. A timely and helpful resource for all in Christian leadership.

SAM GEORGE
Catalyst for Diasporas, Lausanne Movement
Director, Wheaton College Billy Graham Center Global Diaspora Institute

Tim Welch has decades of experience in the Majority World mission field and understands the urgency of reaching the unreached. In order to fulfill the Great Commission in our generation, we must implement effective funding models and finish the task mandated by Christ. I wholeheartedly recommend Tim's insightful book *New Funding Models for Global Mission* for all missionaries and missions agencies.

DAI SUP HAN
Prayer Surge NOW!
AWAKE! Gatherings

By reminding us of Hudson Taylor's statement: "God's work done in God's way will never lack God's supply," Tim Welch invites us from the outset to focus on the owner of it all, before asking us to consider and revisit the various possible funding models for global mission. More than ever, the church in the Majority World has much to contribute when it comes to mission funding and to setting the agenda for global Christianity. Are we doing what we should be doing and going where God is sending with the resources we have? I recommend the reading of this book to all as we seriously consider our participation and partnership in mobilizing resources for the mission entrusted to us by Jesus.

MARIO LI-HING
MANI Leadership Team, AEA Board Chair

This is a very informational and inspirational book for mission workers who want to get creative ideas on how to finance their ministries. May this concise volume help mobilize more workers into the vast harvests among the unreached and unengaged peoples of our world today.

DAVID S. LIM, PhD
Board Chairman, Lausanne Philippines

Our heart for missions cannot be separated from the challenge and privilege of funding missions. The Majority World is producing laborers, a direct answer to the prayer Jesus instructs us to pray (Matt 9:38). Tim Welch makes it clear in this book that sending Kingdom workers to the unreached will be significantly hindered unless we widen our horizons and practice new models of supporting them. He provides a rich list of possibilities to stimulate our thinking, but he offers us much more than pragmatic solutions. His commitment to biblical reflection makes this a valuable and timely read for those who consider the advance of God's Kingdom a high priority.

MUTUA MAHIAINI
International President, The Navigators

This is a timely book that addresses the need for the church in the Majority World to seriously grapple with the issue of mission funding by realizing the tremendous resources and channels for mission support and funding available to the Majority World. I highly commend this book for reading and discussion especially by church and mission leaders in order for more intentional and sustained mission mobilization.

PETER OYUGI
Leadership Team, Movement of African National Initiatives (MANI)

Tim Welch has made a valuable contribution to world missions strategy with this book. This book is particularly important to ministers, such as myself, who serve in the Majority World. The need to effectively mobilize these churches to be self-supporting and be gradually weaned away from exclusively being dependent on foreign contributions is the need of the hour in the ever-changing global scenario. This book is a must read for all engaged in missions all over the world.

REV. LALLIENVEL (LAL) PAKHUONGTE
President, Evangelical Free Church of India

Financing missions is a complex subject. The book opened a new panorama for me, giving me a better idea of the challenges missionaries face and how as a church we can be involved. It is an informative, practical book based on the author's experience and research. Supporting missions should be an item in all church budgets. Also, as a pastor and leader, it has opened up to me new roles I can play in mission involvement.

ISAAC QUINO
Director, Fundación Apoyo, Bolivia

I wish this book would have existed when I began my ministry career. In *New Funding Models for Global Mission*, Tim Welch offers a wonderful gift to the Western church ... if it is willing to accept it. Too often mission leaders rely on funding models for ministry situated in one particular cultural context, to the benefit of primarily dominant-culture Western world ministers. By documenting multitudes of different ways God is funding his mission, Welch shows that there can be a better way. Welch's contribution is helping us to see that funding mission can and is being done in ways that are much closer to God's way than the narrow paradigms we've used in the West. I pray for a massive work of the Spirit through Welch's efforts in this book that we would finally see Western mission learning from and embracing our Majority World brethren. We have so much to learn from them—if we have ears to hear.

ERIC ROBINSON, PhD
Author, "Minister Different" blogs on ministry funding

In 2006, the then International Executive leadership of Operation Mobilization asked me to lead a task team to assist the organization figure out how we do and finance missions differently, especially for our Majority World fields. We recognized that traditional funding models are less effective in the Majority World and that we could not simply "put Saul's armor on David." Tim Welch has a winner here. His well-researched book will be of immense benefit for the whole church, but I would venture, especially for the church in the Majority World. He has come up with practical, implementable suggestions. How we gain and use finance in mission has led to so much heartache in the past for the Majority World, where the issue of money was also a power one. Tim deals well with these aspects. I highly recommend this book.

PETER TARANTAL
Associate International Director, OM
Chair, Majority World Christian Leaders Conversation
Advisor, MANI leadership team

New FUNDINGMODELS for GLOBAL MISSION

Learning from the Majority World

Tim Welch

WILLIAM CAREY PUBLISHING

visit us at missionbooks.org

New Funding Models for Global Mission: Learning from the Majority World

© 2023 by Tim Welch. All Rights Reserved.

No part of this book may be reproduced, stored in a retrieval system, or transmitted in any form or by any means—electronic, mechanical, photocopy, recording, or otherwise—without prior written permission from the publisher, except brief quotations used in connection with reviews in magazines or newspapers. For permission, email permissions@wclbooks.com. For corrections, email editor@wclbooks.com.

All Scripture quotations, unless otherwise indicated, are taken from the Holy Bible, New International Version®, NIV®. Copyright ©1973, 1978, 1984, 2011 by Biblica, Inc.™ Used by permission of Zondervan. All rights reserved worldwide. www.zondervan.com. The "NIV" and "New International Version" are trademarks registered in the United States Patent and Trademark Office by Biblica, Inc.™

Scripture quotations marked (ESV) are from The ESV® Bible (The Holy Bible, English Standard Version®), copyright © 2001 by Crossway, a publishing ministry of Good News Publishers. Used by permission. All rights reserved.

Scripture quotations marked (NLT) are taken from the Holy Bible, New Living Translation, copyright ©1996, 2004, 2015 by Tyndale House Foundation. Used by permission of Tyndale House Publishers, Carol Stream, Illinois 60188. All rights reserved.

Scripture quotations marked (MSG) are taken from *The Message*, copyright © 1993, 2002, 2018 by Eugene H. Peterson. Used by permission of NavPress, represented by Tyndale House Publishers. All rights reserved.

Published by William Carey Publishing
10 W. Dry Creek Cir
Littleton, CO 80120 | www.missionbooks.org

William Carey Publishing is a ministry of Frontier Ventures
Pasadena, CA | www.frontierventures.org

Cover Design: Mike Riester

ISBN: 978-1-64508-471-6 (paperback)
       978-1-64508-473-0 (epub)

Printed Worldwide

27 26 25 24 23   2 3 4 5 6   IN

Library of Congress Control Number: 2023935587

Contents

    A Third Party

    Missionary Pledge Campaigns

    A "Mission Start-Up Group"

    Diaspora Funding

    Tentmakers

    Business as Mission (BAM)

    Partnerships

    Seeking Support from the Mission, Not the Missionary

    Twelve-Church Model

    "Revolving Savings" for Mission

    Crowdfunding

    Living Off the Fruit of Ministry

    Support That Diminishes over Time

    A "Handful of Rice" (*buhfai tham*)

    Part-Time Employment for Spouse

    Reducing Costs

    Endowment Fund

    Supporting a Ministry instead of a Missionary Person/Family

    "Mission Designation"

    Simplified Procedures

    Mission Agencies That Contribute to the Local Church

    Activities and Events

*"God's work done in God's way
will never lack God's supply."*

—Hᴜᴅꜱᴏɴ Tᴀʏʟᴏʀ
missionary to China and founder of the China Inland Mission

Why Study This Topic?

Churches that take the Bible seriously are virtually unanimous in maintaining that Jesus Christ gave a command to all who follow him: a command to make disciples of all nations (Matt 28:19). The Gospels according to Mark and Luke each give a similar command (Mark 16:15; Luke 24:47), and the Gospel according to John treats the same idea by talking about the example of Jesus and his incarnation (John 20:21)—that is, how to send, instead of what to do or say when sending.

Sending people to all the nations in the world supposes that there are sending strategies in place. One school of thought opts for "lay missionaries" (Bjork 2015, 21) to reach the world for Jesus Christ, wanting to move away from mission agencies and toward "tentmakers." Another school of thought accepts the validity of tentmakers while accepting that other models are also valid, thus supporting the validity of mission agencies.

This latter group says that "there is rich biblical and historical precedent for a special commission that is supported [financially] by communities of faith" (Matenga and Gold 2016, 177). But whichever strategy is used, both schools of thought agree that the methods used by the evangelical church in the West to send missionaries are being adopted by the evangelical church in the Majority World. (In this book, I use the term *Majority World* to refer to those countries previously called the "Third World," "developing countries," or the "Global South" by many people today.)

When the Majority World adopts the ways practiced by the West, the financial cost of doing so is quite high. Bonk declares that "the Western missionary enterprise, meanwhile, is utterly and fatally dependent upon the accoutrements of affluence" (Bonk 2006, 18). Can Majority World evangelical churches send their own missionaries while avoiding this dependence on affluence? I believe the answer to this question is yes, provided that these churches are led by transformational leaders.

Transformational leadership aims to impact institutional functions and processes in a way that leads to positive change. This change thereby promotes a holistic transformation of the entire institution as well as the individuals within it. In this case, the institutions concerned are mission agencies and evangelical churches in the Majority World.

Through this book, I hope to contribute to reflective leadership by offering mission and church leaders the opportunity to think differently about the matter of mission funding. I am also seeking to contribute to contextual leadership—helping mission organizations, churches, and their leaders discern what works well and what does not work well in different cultural contexts. Next, this study will contribute to global leadership, because mission agencies and evangelical churches on one continent are different from those on another. Models of mission funding do not have to be the same from one country to the next. Finally, through this book I seek to contribute to prophetic leadership in order to change systems and practices that seem to be failing in their task of resourcing missionaries. Mission agency and church leaders need to consider new possibilities and approaches to global mission funding.

Since the beginning of the "modern era of world mission," toward the end of the eighteenth century and the beginning of the industrialization of Europe, the model most often used for the financing of Western evangelical missionaries has been that of seeking financial support "by faith." In other words, the missionary himself or herself has to go from church to church or person to person to ask for some kind of financial partnership. This was not—and still is not—the model used by all church denominations in the West, but it is the model used by many evangelical churches around the world.

I know from personal experience that some evangelical churches which have formed their own mission agencies, such as the Baptist General Conference Church and the Conservative Baptist Church, both in the United States, ask their missionaries to pass from church to church, seeking to supplement their financial support. This demonstrates that these church denominations are not able to support their missionaries solely through their offerings, as churches have done in the past and as other Protestant and Catholic churches do today.

This model of seeking financial support "by faith" certainly has some advantages. One advantage is that missionaries know their donors personally and receive increased prayer support as a result. This may help to explain why this model has been used for over two hundred years in the evangelical community. Such longevity explains why I refer to it as the "traditional" model. However, it is based on certain presuppositions that are necessary for it to succeed.

Borthwick quotes Pastor Oscar Muriu of Nairobi Chapel, who says that this model depends on a fairly high economic level, financial stability, and disposable income in the country where the missionary resides (Borthwick 2012). In addition, it requires the cultural acceptance of approaching potential donors to ask for money for one's ministry. That and many other factors will be addressed in later chapters.

With the publication of Philip Jenkins's book *The Next Christendom*, in 2002, the Christian world became more aware that the Majority World includes more Christians than all the countries of Europe and North America combined. The fact that Christianity is truly a world religion helps explain why churches in the Majority World seek to be a part of God's global mission. Increasingly, missionaries come from Asia, Africa, and South America, rather than only from so-called "Western" countries.

Despite the rich missionary history of the Christian church—Protestant, Catholic, and Orthodox—and their various ways of funding missionaries, evangelical mission agencies and churches tend to focus on one model of seeking financial support for their missionaries. Again, I call this the traditional model—i.e., where the missionary seeks his or her own funding. Perhaps the relative success of this model in the Western world makes it seem like the best model to use. But mission agencies from the evangelical tradition need to recognize that other models are equally effective.

I know an Ivorian missionary who serves with a US-based mission agency, and that agency has forbidden him to use any other model for seeking financial support; he must use this traditional model in which he has to go from church to church and person to person to ask for an ongoing contribution to his funding. He even talked with some of his leaders to contend that other models would be more effective in Africa, but they refused to change their approach to mission funding. At least my friend has the advantage of holding a leadership position in his organization, which means that he travels to the United States from time to time for meetings and then visits new acquaintances to tell them about his need for support. Most of his African colleagues don't have that opportunity.

Unfortunately, the traditional funding model has the potential to negatively impact missionary workers around the world. According to Pastor Muriu's remarks cited above, this model prevents many people from acquiring adequate mission funding because their social standing means that they don't know enough people with sufficient disposable income to contribute to their ministry in this way. And these people don't have disposable income because their country's economy is neither prosperous nor stable.

The consequences of this situation are that the missionary workforce in our world is in danger of becoming solely white—which doesn't properly reflect the global body of Christ at all, and which in turn risks communicating that Christianity is *not* for all cultures and all peoples of the world.

The traditional model of missionary funding also frightens many Christians who wonder if they should consider becoming missionaries. This is true not only in the Majority World, but in Western countries as well. Younger generations resist the idea of "begging" for their monthly financial support. Although this fear of raising financial support is not justified biblically, it is a widespread impression among missionary children. And if this causes fear among the children of Western missionaries, it is all the more true for young Christians in the Majority World who do not dare experiment with this model.

So that leads us to the basic question of this book: Apart from the so-called "traditional" model, what other models of missionary financial support might be more appropriate and suitable for evangelical mission agencies and churches in Majority World countries?

As mentioned above, the traditional model of fundraising requires missionaries themselves to go from church to church or person to person to request some sort of regular financial partnership. This model was well suited to the nineteenth century, when several "parachurch" mission agencies emerged, such as the China Inland Mission (now Overseas Missionary Fellowship) and the Worldwide Evangelization Crusade founded in England, the Sudan Interior Mission founded in Canada, and many others later. Since these mission agencies were not linked to a single Christian denomination, it may have made more sense for their members to travel from church to church in order to find their financial support.

Today, however, with the proliferation of mission agencies and parachurch associations and the decline in the number of churches that take the Bible seriously in this regard, this model risks flooding churches in the evangelical tradition with its growing demands.

So are there other models to use?

The answer to that question is yes, and the overall purpose of this book is to identify and analyze the other financial support models for global mission funding that evangelical mission agencies and churches in the Majority World have used. I hope to facilitate participation by the Majority World church in global mission by listing these other funding models and thus help churches see that possibilities more appropriate to their context exist. New models that are better suited to the situation in which the Majority World church finds itself will provide more adequate funding for global mission, because it is clear that certain deficiencies exist in the area of mission funding in evangelical churches. At the same time, the Western church will do well to learn from these models which the Majority World church is already using.

Chapter 2

Missionary Funding Past and Present

Before we try to solve a problem, first we need to understand the context. Otherwise we risk creating other problems with our proposed solution. In this chapter I will survey the history of mission funding and then focus on the current situation in Majority World churches. And then, in later chapters, I will look at some proposed solutions.

The Christian church has been sending out missionaries since the beginning of its existence. Acts 13 recounts the apostles Barnabas and Saul/ Paul being sent out by the church at Antioch. And even before that, in Acts 11, we see that "men from Cyprus and Cyrene" (v. 20) went as missionaries to Antioch. However, these texts do not explain the means used to finance these various journeys. Later it is clear that the Apostle Paul at times lived at his own expense, working "night and day" as a tentmaker "in order not to be a burden to anyone" (1 Thess 2:9)—i.e., so as not to burden financially those he sought to reach with the message of the gospel.

At the same time, some local churches had decided to support those who were leaving their homes to serve as evangelists and missionaries (see, for example, Phil 4:15, 16; 3 John 5–8). Sometimes churches that Paul had founded helped him financially (see 2 Cor 11:8, 9; Phil 4:10–20), and sometimes a church that Paul had not yet visited helped him with his mission (see Rom 15:24). More details on these points will be given in chapter 8. But in general, it seems that at times local churches financed those who left their homes to serve as missionaries, and at other times the missionaries themselves met their own material needs by working on the mission field.

In the first and second centuries AD, the church was still pondering this question of how to support those who travelled to spread the gospel message. The Didache, a book of Christian instruction written during that time, taught that an apostle or prophet who asked for money was a fake; if he asked for more than bread for his journey or for lodging that exceeded two days, he was a false prophet (see the Didache, chapter XI, verses 5 and 6). This shows that the church at that time did not envision distant missionary journeys, despite the biblical evidence of this kind of journey made on several occasions by the Apostle Paul.

Nevertheless, it is very interesting to note that the Didache said that Christians should offer the firstfruits of their agricultural produce and livestock to the prophets, "for they are your high priests. But if you have not a prophet, give to the poor" (chapter XIII, verses 3 and 4). This teaching might indicate that the church at that time emphasized the importance of mission, even at the expense of the poor, and even if this mission was only more or less local. Providing for the material needs of God's servants remained an important part of the early church, even though other influential church leaders—such as Lactantius of North Africa and later Basil of Caesarea—taught that believers should give only from their surplus to meet the legitimate needs of the poor or the prophets (González 2002).

With Emperor Theodosius establishing Christianity as the official religion of the Roman Empire in the year 380, the church increasingly appropriated its power and wealth for missions, but worldliness also crept into its use of money. Some bishops, such as Wulfila (also called Ulfilas), went out to evangelize the Germanic tribes. Being Goth himself, Wulfila's "vigorous evangelism was only too successful, and he and many of his people eventually moved to form a Gothic enclave within the [Roman] Empire" (Walls 1996, 38).

Quite a number of Christians, however, decided to flee the worldly influence that existed in the empire, and hence monasticism was born. Over time monasteries were established, becoming centers of both piety and education. It is not surprising that these places later became the cradle of mission for many centuries. In the fifth century the English monk Patrick evangelized the Celtic people in Ireland and subsequently founded a large number of monasteries there. Nicole (1972) states that Irish monasteries were centers of culture, piety, and missionary activity. Ireland became the base for evangelizing Great Britain (England, Scotland, Wales). Irish and British monks later evangelized the European continent and established monasteries in Germany, Switzerland, and northern Italy. These monasteries became centers of evangelism and education.

During this same period, the Roman Catholic Church used various religious orders to win others to the faith. Benedict of Nursia, for example, founded a monastic movement; and his followers, who were called Benedictines, went out to evangelize. Eventually they spread throughout Western Europe. In 596, Pope Gregory I sent about forty Benedictine monks to England under the leadership of the priest Augustine of Canterbury, who was able to convert King Ethelbert. The Catholic Church had the funds to finance these evangelistic missions, and the popes used religious orders to send their members to foreign lands.

Once established, the order usually followed the rule *ora et labora* ("pray and work") (Ravitz 2010, para. 4). Even though some religious orders later followed the example of the Catholic Church and fell into worldliness, new orders were born, such as the Cistercians, Augustinians, Dominicans, and Franciscans. They followed the same model in regard to financing mission; and the last three groups mentioned, as mendicant orders, used the additional means of begging to add to their income.

Starting with the Reformation, world mission was more or less neglected for two centuries, at least on the Protestant side. In the eighteenth century the Moravians, who lived in modern-day Czechia, sent missionaries to the Caribbean islands. Since the Moravians represented a fairly small evangelical movement, these missionaries went out as "tentmakers." Once they arrived in the New World, they had to look for or create work to feed themselves and meet their daily needs. Later some Moravians went to reside in the English colony of Pennsylvania, where their "agricultural and industrial economy" was well known (Moravian Church in America 2018, para. 12). Their work benefited the local people as they preached the gospel to them. This model was also used by the Massachusetts Bay Colony and the Basel Mission Trading Company (Steffen and Barnett 2006).

This confirms what Bakke has said about work: "Business and other secular work is both a mission … and a mission field" (Bakke 2005, 275). Thus, for more than a thousand years the financing of mission, as practiced by the religious orders of the Catholic Church or by Protestant groups, was based on work done by missionaries on the mission field. It is not surprising, therefore, to read Bjork's conclusion in this regard that "the funding of 'full-time' missionaries is, in fact, a historical anomaly" (Bjork 2015, 36) and that the church needs to reassess the value of lay missionaries in order to better understand both the purpose and the funding of mission.

This brings us to the "modern era of world mission" mentioned above. In 1793, William Carey went to India as a missionary. Some churches at that time did not value mission, believing that God's election made mission unnecessary or even counter to God's will. Thus, they did not agree to finance such a missionary expedition. So Carey worked on site in India, first in an indigo factory and later as a teacher (Johnson 2014). But his treatise entitled *An Enquiry into the Obligations of Christians to Use Means for the Conversion of the Heathens* was widely distributed, essentially launching the missionary movement in England at the end of the eighteenth century. Carey spoke of the use of financial means to achieve this goal.

Walls (1996, 246) comments:

> It is significant that Carey—a man of the provinces and of humble station—takes his analogy from commerce; organizing a [missionary] society is something like floating a company. He is looking for the appropriate means to accomplish a task which cannot be accomplished through the usual machinery of the Church.

Although Carey himself did not receive much funding in this way, his idea of this new model undeniably altered the future of global mission. Missiologist Timothy Tennent (2010, 261) argues that Carey, the "father" of modern mission, based his thinking on a business model:

> Carey, as a Protestant rejecting the Catholic, monastic forms of mission, had no ecclesiastical structures to look to for guidance. So, he proposed a mission society based largely upon the model of secular trading societies, which were being organized for commercial purposes.

Two mission agencies, the Church Missionary Society—formed by the evangelical branch of the Anglican Church, and the London Missionary Society, formed by the evangelical branch of the Church of England Dissidents—were modelled on the structure Carey had proposed. In addition, an American mission agency—the American Board of Commissioners for Foreign Mission—was established in 1810, following the same business model as their "sister organizations" across the Atlantic. According to

Anderson (1987, 67) some key members of the Congregationalist Church determined that

> if a foreign mission were to be anything but a pious hope, a foreign missionary organization had to be formed to popularize the idea, raise money, disburse it, select missionaries, assign them to stations, support them and supervise their activities.

Bessenecker concludes that the result was "a missionary corporation, a Christian version of the for-profit trading company" (2014a, loc. 413). Later he adds that the "American missionary corporation was desperately dependent on the financial resources of external investors for success" (2014a, loc. 450).

All of this briefly explains how the "traditional" model of mission financing came into being in England and later in America. To this day this model has changed little in the evangelical church in the Western world. Outside persons almost always finance people who leave the Western world to become "missionaries." These missionaries—at least those who are Protestant— usually join their denomination's mission agency or an interdenominational mission agency instead of being sent abroad by their own congregation, although some Protestant churches send their missionaries themselves. This traditional model dominates the current Western scene in terms of financing Protestant mission.

However, the World Christian Database at the Center for the Study of Global Christianity, linked to Gordon-Conwell Theological Seminary, estimates that there were 440,000 expatriate Christian missionaries in the world in 2018. This figure includes missionaries from all Christian traditions (Johnson, Zurlo, Hickman, and Crossing 2018). Other sources estimate that there are only 140,000 Protestant missionaries worldwide (The Traveling Team, n.d.). This means that there are approximately 300,000 missionaries in the world who come from the Catholic Church, the Orthodox Church, or another Christian tradition. It is likely that these other missionaries are supported financially by their churches, since the traditional model of seeking support is not often practiced by non-Protestants. So the challenge of financing Christian missionaries seems to be more of a Protestant issue, and especially an evangelical church matter, than a universal challenge for the Christian church.

This overview from biblical times to the present day demonstrates that other models of missionary funding have been used in the past and are still in use today, but that evangelical churches tend to opt for the traditional model based on a business model. By limiting themselves in this way, mission agencies run certain risks, risks that will be discussed in the next chapter, which asks, "What's at stake?"

Chapter 3

What's at Stake?

Every decision you make has consequences. Sometimes these consequences are fortunate, and sometimes they're not. In the latter case, it would have been better to consider the bad consequences before arriving at your decision; in the former case, it would be good to think about the good consequences even if it is after the fact. In regard to missionary financing, the stakes are high, since several aspects of world evangelism depend on it; so we need to think through our funding decisions carefully.

It would be an exaggeration to say that the question of missionary financing will be the most significant matter facing the future of Christianity. After all, factors such as world politics, economics, technology, and even climate will have their say regarding the number of people who will leave their countries to become missionaries. However, this issue of funding will play a major role in future global mission, since it affects the church's vision and methods for reaching the two-thirds of the world's population that does not yet know the Lord Jesus Christ. Without a better answer to the question of how to finance mission, many people may not fully understand, or even hear, the message of salvation.

One limitation with the traditional model of missionary fundraising is that funds must normally first pass through the local sending church, its headquarters, or the mission agency, which collects the funds and then distributes them to the missionaries each month. This process works well for individuals working in countries that are open to missionaries. But restricted countries don't accept people who come as missionaries, and they often don't accept people funded by Christian organizations. The paper trail for such a person's salary would be difficult to hide. That is why Thomas Sudyk says that "in these restricted countries, *traditional mission methods are obsolete*" (Yamamori and Eldred 2003, 156; emphasis added), while models such as "business as mission" are readily accepted by host cultures.

The traditional model, in both its structure and its methods, undermines the scope of global mission in the future, reducing the number of countries that will accept such "workers." But if these workers are normally employed by a commercial company or social organization, their source of income is not immediately suspect. Moreover, the door will open more naturally for these workers to work in an area of social concern, even in a restricted country.

Glenn Smith reminds us that mission is linked to incarnation, which cannot be dissociated from spirituality, and "spirituality cannot be dissociated from the quest for justice, from accompanying the poor and oppressed or from defending their rights" (Smith 2009, 4). A worker's source of income is linked to his or her field of action; unlinking one can enlarge the other. That is, a salaried worker from an NGO can have a greater social impact on a community than a missionary who does not have the same access to these people because he is not part of an organization recognized by the community.

A second area of concern is the effectiveness of the traditional model in the Majority World. If this model does not generate sufficient funds, the number of missionaries sent will decrease significantly. A number of authors have expressed their reluctance in this regard. For example, João Mordomo, from Brazil, says that the traditional model—what he calls the "Professional Missionary Model" (Steffen and Barnett 2006, 224)—"runs a significant risk of never achieving critical financial mass" (Steffen and Barnett, 225).

Jonathan Lewis, who has worked in Latin America, says that "It has yet to be demonstrated that the typical North American and European model of church-based support is a solution for funding the Argentine missions movement" (Pate 1989, 105). Numerous authors maintain that many models and new models of funding need to be used to better send out missionaries from the Majority World; and they have been making this argument for several decades, as well as more recently (Clark 1971; Wong 1973; Keyes 1983; Bush 1990; Lederleitner 2010; Doyle 2015).

Although these alternative ideas have been expressed for a long time, the traditional model still dominates in the minds of many mission agencies. However, the inefficiency of this model could prevent the sending of large numbers of missionaries. For example, one Latino missionary, using the pseudonym L, reports that in using the traditional model of fundraising during his eight years as a missionary among college students, he spent only three years in ministry and five years seeking financial support (L 2014). If a model prevents a servant from serving for much of his or her time due to a lack of finances, it may be time to change models.

One might even wonder if this model creates a certain fear among the churches in the Majority World, since they see only the exorbitant price of sending a Western family to the mission field. Compared to the budgets of these Western missionaries, a pastor could conclude that his church would never find such a great amount of money to send one of their families to the mission field. And even if they were to raise that much money, he may then fear that his own salary will decrease later on as a result.

This situation only reinforces the spirit of poverty that is already present in the Majority World. Even when a church wants to participate in global mission, it wonders how it can do so. The financial obstacles seem insurmountable. Or worse, in the long run an unintended consequence of this spirit of poverty is that it kills the local church's vision for global mission. The stakes surrounding mission funding are high. Fear, poverty, and the death of the global vision should not be what happens when we talk about mission.

If the model used in fundraising is not changed, the stakes will not only be limited to what has been discussed above. Another issue will be in regard to the actual persons going out as missionaries—that is, missionaries will predominantly be white people from Europe and North America. The Pew Research Center reports that in the United States "the median wealth of white households is twenty times that of black households and eighteen times that of Hispanic households" (Pew Research Center 2011, 1). A similar article on missionary funding explains that Asian missionaries are 2.5 times more likely than whites to say that their families are embarrassed by a child having to raise funds for support (Perry 2012).

If this is the case in the United States, where the traditional model is widely accepted, what is the potential for success in the Majority World, where this model is barely known? Eric Robinson concludes that the barriers to this model are insurmountable for non-whites for two reasons: "structural disadvantages" (Robinson 2014a, para. 7) and "cultural barriers" (para. 11). As these quotations show, some ethnic groups have no disposable income to give toward missions due to a lack of means, and others don't easily accept the traditional model, which, in their opinion, is too similar to begging.

Thus, this model favors white missionaries, and such a result hinders the effectiveness of world mission. Scott Bessenecker agrees when he asks, "Is there something about how Protestant mission is shaped that makes it easier for white folk to enter and more difficult for others?" (Bessenecker 2014a, loc. 254). Even in South Korea, an economically advanced country, Steve Sang-Cheol Moon says that it is very difficult for new missionaries to mobilize the necessary financial support. His conclusion: "The future of Korean mission finance does not look bright" (Moon 2013, 142).

Another finding is that the traditional model fosters individualism. The missionary is responsible for his or her own fundraising, and the local church of some missionaries plays almost no role in sending them abroad. Too often this model emphasizes the relationship between the mission agency and the individual who is going to the mission field; the local church is left out. Robinson (2014b, para. 19) says,

> We need to ask ourselves, is the "every staff for themselves" paradigm of personal support raising really compatible with the shared relationships we see modelled in the Godhead or even Paul's description of the Church as the interdependent members of Christ's body?

Everywhere in the Bible we see a greater emphasis on the community than on the individual, and this is also true in many cultures of the Majority World. However, the traditional fundraising model tends to run counter to this community principle. It places more emphasis on independence than on interdependence, more on the individual than on the community. Bessenecker is even more negative about this tendency, saying: "Interdependence is the chief vision for human relationships. ... Independence is a grotesque malfunction of our design" (Bessenecker 2014a, loc. 2509).

The stakes are therefore numerous: restricted countries that refuse missionaries may also refuse those who want to enter as "lay people" because of their method of financing, not only reducing the number of countries that will accept workers for the Lord, but also limiting the social or economic benefit they can offer. A second challenge is that, due to the traditional fundraising model, the number of missionaries sent may drop because of a lack of financial resources resulting from this method.

This model is decreasingly effective in the Western world, according to Bessenecker (2014a), and it is likely to be even less effective in the Majority World. Thirdly, the impact of this model on the church in the Majority World is becoming dangerous. Fear and a spirit of poverty can kill the church's vision. Fourth, the gospel message risks being misunderstood if the messengers are predominantly white. This is already the case in Africa, where many Africans, especially Muslims, believe that Christianity is a white man's religion.

The ethnicity of the missionaries influences the impact of the mission; and if the models allowed more people from the Majority World to become messengers, this would positively influence the message. Thus the Christian message itself is at stake. And fifth, if an individualistic strategy is effective in finding financial support, such as with the traditional model, missionaries will be tempted to think that this same strategy will bear fruit in ministry on the mission field. Teamwork and what it means to be a Christian leader are two areas that are likely to suffer from this model that emphasizes individualism.

All of these factors together make this topic of mission funding quite critical to the future of global mission, although other important factors have not been included in this discussion. The stakes will be high if this issue of appropriate financial models is not resolved. But if evangelical churches in the Majority World can focus more on appropriate means of mission funding, it will give them the opportunity to contribute more effectively and more faithfully to world mission. The Western church can learn from the Majority World in asking whether there are more appropriate models to use, even if the traditional model is not to be abandoned. Majority World leaders will participate all the more with God in his mission, and it is this topic that we will examine in chapter 5, after a brief discussion of the traditional model in chapter 4.

Chapter 4

Mission Funding 1.0—Pros and Cons

The traditional model, in which the missionary seeks his own financial support by finding sponsors from churches, friends, and relatives, has been predominant in the evangelical milieu for more than two hundred years. While other valid models exist and should be used, this one should not be abandoned. Its greatest advantage is that it produces a strong bond between the missionary and the donor, and the result is increased spiritual support (especially through prayer) from those who contribute financially as opposed to those who do not, because the former are more "invested" in the ministry.

It goes without saying that much of the literature on missionary funding speaks of this traditional model of missionary fundraising. These books explain the importance of personal relationships in discussions with potential donors, or the biblical basis for asking others to participate in a ministry, or even methods for presenting the total mission budget and how to achieve it. Of course, they all talk about the importance of prayer and perseverance. Dozens of books deal with these different aspects of seeking financial support when an individual or family embarks on a mission.

But very few books or articles talk about models that are more appropriate for the Majority World. Apart from books that deal with those who want to become tentmakers or to practice their profession abroad, it is implied in the literature that the missionary will seek his/her necessary funding before going to the mission field.

I call this traditional approach Mission Funding 1.0. A typical example of this kind of book is Scott Morton's *Funding Your Ministry: A Field Guide for Raising Personal Support* (2017). This book covers biblical principles for fundraising; how to develop a fundraising strategy; how to ask for a contribution by phone, face-to-face, or in front of a church; the importance of a good relationship with a donor; writing interesting prayer letters; proper management of money received, and so on.

In addition, Morton has a blog where he talks about topics such as year-end fundraising, asking for specific amounts, approaching past donors, and other similar topics. In other words, all his ideas revolve around the principle that missionaries must do the fundraising themselves. It is true that in the third edition of his book, Morton acknowledges that these practices must be "modified to suit each situation" (Morton 2017, xi), including other cultures, but he still focuses on the traditional model where the missionary is responsible for finding the necessary funds for his ministry.

In all fairness to Morton, he also wrote a book called *Blind Spots: Leading Your Team & Ministry to Full Funding*. There, he speaks of other fundraising models, such as business as mission, tentmaking, having a spouse work, living off of one's own investments, and working with a mission or church that guarantees a salary. He also addresses some of the downsides to raising personal support, including how much time support raising takes away from ministry, the fact that donors from cultures without a history of monthly support often give only one-off gifts or nothing at all, and how staff from non-evangelical backgrounds struggle to create a large mailing list of potential donors. So Morton does not ignore the problems that individual fundraising can present. However, he does not go into any detail as to how best to find solutions to those problems. He concludes (2016 loc. 1359) by saying that he encourages missionaries to objectively ask themselves:

In my context, what method of funding best advances the gospel? Your comfort is not the issue. Your preference on fundraising is not the issue. The deciding factor is: What advances the gospel best?

This book is an attempt to find appropriate answers to that question for missionaries from the Majority World. Most likely, missionaries will find several answers, and not just one, that fit their situation the best.

Interestingly, David Clines (2006), who served in Honduras, proposed that the traditional model be used *more often* in fundraising in his church. He came from a church where the entire church denomination sought funds for missionaries through special offerings. But in his view, this practice neglected the relational aspect that was so prevalent and important in churches in Latin America, and that is why he preferred the traditional model.

While acknowledging the truth of his observation, it should be added that this would be especially true for Latin American countries that are sufficiently wealthy, which is not the case everywhere and is not even really the case in Honduras. Other models will have their place, as Latin American and Anglo-American authors (L 2014; Otaola 2014; Robinson 2014b) speak of the difficulty for Latin American missionaries to find funds in the United States using this model.

Some authors look beyond the traditional model and propose other solutions to the problems of missionary funding. George Verwer, the director of Operation Mobilisation, spoke of other funding models, all the while maintaining that the traditional model can continue and that those who choose it should "expect to be funded willingly and cheerfully by individuals and churches, without shame and with a sense that as laborers in God's work they are worthy of their wages" (Verwer 2000, 119). Verwer's approach is broader than Morton's, because he proposes the adoption of several models at the same time, rather than focusing on only one at the expense of the others. This perspective is more promising in regard to the future of global mission and the issue of mission funding.

Although many writers see the traditional model as having weaknesses, few authors have been openly critical of it. But over time, this is beginning to change. Paul Borthwick, after giving the financial criteria necessary for this model to succeed, clearly states, "The [Majority World] cannot afford this model" (Borthwick 2012, 172).

João Mordomo (Steffen and Barnett, 2006) believes that this model does not produce the desired results in countries that are part of the emerging missions movement. And Scott Bessenecker (2014a) is perhaps the most resolute of critics in saying that this model is based on a history that is much more commercial and secular than "missional" and biblical, a model created in a Western context that does not apply well to the global situation.

Bessenecker is mostly against the traditional model because he maintains that in general this model is not "biblical" or theologically faithful. He sees commercial and cultural elements in it; he holds that this model is based on independence instead of biblical interdependence. I respect his point of view. Opinions are rather divided, however, as to what is truly "biblical" in the world of mission finance. For example, Scott Morton (2017) is a strong advocate of the traditional model and uses biblical principles to explain it to others.

Verwer (2000), who is a mission director, speaks of other models in addition to the traditional model, suggesting that he accepts the traditional model as sufficiently "biblical." David Bjork (2015) speaks against the traditional model as not being biblical, but for reasons other than those Bessenecker gives. Bessenecker accepts the idea that a person can be a "full-time" missionary, but he prefers to use other models of mission funding. Bjork, on the other hand, does not accept the idea that a "full-time" missionary is an essentially biblical model.

Due to such a diversity of views on what is "biblical" and what is not, I have chosen not to enter into this debate, preferring rather to discuss each model in terms of its utility. Of course, we are not dealing with practices that are downright anti-biblical, such as bank robbery, as a model of missionary financing! But apart from this reservation, I will not enter into the debate as to which models are more "biblical" than others.

Bessenecker, Bjork, and Robinson are the three authors who question the traditional model the most intelligently and rigorously. They examine rather meticulously the negative side of the traditional model, especially with regard to missionaries who come from ethnic minorities. They do not hesitate to think outside the box. Bessenecker, in particular, asks pertinent questions about the cultural and historical role of the traditional model. He says (2014a loc. 3032–40) that he would like our world to resemble the world in the New Testament:

> A world where prisoners and prostitutes, outcasts and oppressed occupy the seats of honor. These are Christianity's new architects. They are the experts at the center of God's Kingdom, and they live and work at the fulcrum of the twenty-first century church. We would be foolish not to invite them to assist us in the process of deconstructing the industrial complex and reconstructing the ancient, lighter form of church and mission.

It is time for the Protestant church and its mission to overturn the tables of the corporate worldview that has held our imaginations hostage. It is time to re-envision a mission designed for the twenty-first century. And while new structures and new workers from the margins will certainly have their own liabilities and cultural blinders, they must become co-creators of a new season of mission.

Bjork begins his argument with the great international missionary conference that took place in Edinburgh, Scotland, in 1910, where the organizers wanted to mobilize "full-time" missionaries at the expense of "lay" missionaries. He examines several New Testament texts to show that Paul's "normal" missionary practice was to support himself financially. As a result of his study, he concludes that "the missionary model we have adopted since Edinburgh, and which is being followed by churches in the southern hemisphere, is largely flawed" (Bjork 2015, 36).

Robinson (2014c) says that the men of Cyprus and Cyrene in Acts 11 were pioneers in sharing the gospel with non-Jews. These minority and bicultural men served as a bridge between cultures because they were accustomed to doing so. The Spirit of God used them to lead the church into a new era, one in which people were moving from a Jewish sect to "Christians" for the first time. Robinson says that the Spirit wants to do the same thing again today, using bicultural ethnic minorities as a bridge between the old and new contexts of mobilizing for mission.

Based on the Scriptures, these authors show that what works for one culture does not necessarily have to be exported to other cultures. The church in each era must reevaluate the methods to be used, both in the church and in mission. These six authors mentioned—Verwer, Borthwick, Mordomo, Bessenecker, Bjork, and Robinson—express this truth very clearly. We can build on their example, and chapter 6 will give some ideas to start with. But before we get there, we will look at some modifications that could be made to the traditional model.

Tweaking Tradition

Even if the traditional model has enough positive aspects to merit its continued use, its implementation can be modified. Here are *three* ways to put this model into practice in a local church. And there may be additional variations for doing so as well.

1) After being solicited by a mission agency or missionary, the local church may create a budget line for mission, and a specific agency or missionary may indeed benefit from that budget. The advantage of this approach is that the recipient knows in advance how much money will be received each month or quarter. In addition, it is more in line with the expectations of pastors, who seem to prefer that the missionary receive a regular income instead of seeking their support on their own (Welch 2019).

Pastor Meshak Rurangwa states that every year his Good Shepherd Church in Nairobi, Kenya, "budgets for missions and contributes part of the normal offering for that purpose" (*AfriGo* June 2022, 7). If only more churches would follow this example, it would be such an encouragement for global mission in the Majority World.

A disadvantage, however, is that this method tends to "hide" mission from local church members, as budget expenditures are rarely discussed from the pulpit. If a church adopts this method of funding mission, it will be necessary to communicate clearly so the congregation knows who is supported by the church and what their ministries entail, even if the actual support figures remain confidential and only the overall part of the budget designated for mission is communicated. Otherwise members of the congregation won't even be aware of their own church's missionary commitment.

2) A local church may make a regular donation to a missionary or mission agency, but this donation can remain outside the church budget if it comes from a special offering each quarter or from an income-generating activity. Some churches prefer this approach because the funds donated to the mission remain outside the budget and do not, at least in theory, affect the usual tithes and offerings received by the local church.

The disadvantage of this approach is that the missionary recipients never know how much money will be collected each time, making it more difficult for them to set their own budgets. But depending on the local church, sometimes such offerings are more generous than a budget line, as they are less "hidden" from church members. Usually the results of such special offerings are announced publicly. We should also note that the personal relationship between a missionary and a local church is important in such cases, and that matters to many people in the Majority World. The better known the missionary, the greater the special offering for his or her ministry.

3) A variation of these two approaches exists when a mission agency approaches a church denomination and establishes a good relationship with it. The church commits itself to support a number of the mission agency's missionaries or projects for a certain period of time. This can be done by including the mission in the budget, or through outside-the-budget offerings.

This approach is quite popular in Nigeria, according to discussions with Reuben Ezemadu, who has employed this strategy for the Christian Missionary Foundation. Often a mission agency leader comes to a church service to talk about the various ministries that his mission is carrying out. The result is that funds for missionaries as well as funds for the operational costs of the agency are received.

In all three cases mentioned, it is the missionary or mission agency that initiates contact with the local church or its denominational administration. The responsibility for fundraising still rests with the recipient of the funds. And it is precisely this aspect of the traditional model that creates a problem for many missionaries in the Majority World, because it is culturally wrong to ask for money for oneself. Thus some modifications to this model could make it more practical for missionaries from the Majority World.

A Third Party

When using the traditional model, a third party could seek financial support on behalf of the missionary. For example, a leader from the mission field could send letters or emails, make phone calls, or prepare a video conference call on behalf of the missionary who will be coming to that field; or a mission agency's field leader could visit a few churches in the missionary's home country or even elsewhere to present the financial needs of the missionary; or a pastor who knows the missionary candidate quite well could speak to other pastors on behalf of the missionary, opening the door into other local churches. The Apostle Paul often advocated on behalf of his teammates (see, for example, Rom 16:2; 1 Cor 16:11; Titus 3:13, 14). The advantage of this approach over the traditional model is that the missionary avoids the impression of being selfish or of begging, since she is not asking for funds for herself.

It is also possible for friends attending another church to ask their pastors if their friend, who is a missionary candidate, could come and present his ministry to the local church. If so, the friends should agree to present the financial component to the church in favor of the missionary candidate. In that way, the missionary avoids asking directly for money for himself.

The use of a third party in favor of missionaries is a fairly common practice in evangelical churches in the Majority World. My research shows that 75 percent of mission agencies report that their missionaries have such "advocates" or "stakeholders" (Welch 2019). This is very practical, because not all the fundraising work falls on one person. In addition, these third-party advocates can easily become the nucleus of a mission start-up group (see page 29) in a local church with experience in advocating for a missionary.

A mission in Ethiopia established a whole network of mission mobilizers—that is, third-party representatives with the very specific purpose of motivating others for world mission. Still another mission served as a third party by publishing a prayer booklet for unreached peoples that it circulates among evangelical churches (Welch 2019, 166). These examples show the advantages of third parties in mission funding in the Majority World, and churches in the West would do well to foster the same spirit of having third-party advocates for their missionaries.

In 2021 a missionary from Peru, Juanita, held some fundraising events via Zoom (due to the COVID-19 pandemic) prior to going to Thailand. She not only had someone from her mission organization talk about her upcoming ministry in Thailand, but she actually had her future Thai language teacher join the call and talk about life in Thailand, with someone translating into Spanish for the listeners.

This same teacher, who is not yet a Christian, joined Juanita for several subsequent Zoom calls, since she was glad to tell about her country. As a result, the listeners in these various meetings got more excited because they heard from someone in the field country with whom Juanita would be interacting. Juanita's creativity in recruiting a third party from her field of ministry resulted in a larger number of people signing up to join her financial support team and to pray for her ministry in Thailand.

Missionary Pledge Campaigns

After being contacted by a missionary, a local church might agree to help out financially. However, it may not be able to do so, other than to take up a special offering once or twice a year. But, as mentioned above, this can make the missionary's life more difficult, since he or she will never know how much money will be received from the church. So to remedy this problem, a local church can start what is called a "missionary pledge campaign."

In such a campaign, each person or family who wants to support a missionary financially will ask God to help them know how much money to pledge. Then they will fill out a card or booklet to indicate the amount of money that they will give, by faith, in a year—either to the mission agency or to the individual missionary. This is an effective way to find regular donors. A church leader will receive the money each time and mark each contribution on the person's card or in their booklet to help them track their progress toward the pledge.

Churches in Ethiopia, such as the Kale Heywet Church and the Mekane Yesu Church, are using this model with great success. These financial pledges are in addition to the usual tithes and offerings, and this aspect must be clearly communicated to the congregation. The advantage of this approach over occasional special offerings is that the missionary will have an idea in advance as to the amount of financial support that will come in each month or quarter, assuming that members remain more or less faithful to their pledges.

A "Mission Start-Up Group"

Related to these concepts is the idea of establishing a mission start-up group (MSG) in the local congregation. Such a group, which is different than an evangelism committee, can play a critical role in mission. Glenn Smith writes about the problem of the privatization of faith that dominates so many Western churches. He notes that a specific Christian in a church is not an isolated person, but rather a person "within a community of fellow followers of Jesus" (Smith 2017, 8). The local church should participate, as a community, in God's mission.

The MSG is comprised of a small group of people who have a heart for mission, a group that helps the local church participate in God's mission on a practical level. These people will make the church members aware of world mission, unreached countries and peoples, missionary prayer topics familiar to the church, denominational missions and relief efforts, etc. The members of this group will keep the missionary vision before their local church.

They will also be responsible for the logistics of a missionary family returning for home assignment. In addition, they may be useful for fundraising during the missionary pledge campaigns mentioned earlier and for sending funds to missionaries or their agencies. They can also be used as a third party to speak on behalf of a missionary candidate.

Having an MSG made up of people who are enthusiastic about mission can completely change the atmosphere in a church, helping it to have a vision that goes beyond its own city or even its own country. These people, who function as a "mission start-up," are helpful in creating a truly global vision in a local church. David Clines (2006) emphasized this idea in mobilizing Christians in Honduras, and Reuben Ezemadu (2005) did the same for churches in Nigeria.

Diaspora Funding

Another tweak of the traditional model is to seek financial support from people in the diaspora—that is, people from a certain country who now live outside their home country. Instead of approaching a local church for support, a missionary approaches a group of people—often in the form of a cultural association—who live in another country. If interested, these people make a financial commitment to support a specific missionary or ministry in their home country.

This kind of funding is more effective for projects than for regular support of a missionary, since there is often a desire to do something concrete and positive for their homeland. Christians are often a part of these national associations abroad, and missionaries can contact them to assist in funding their ministry. It should not be forgotten that individual contributions made by people from the African Diaspora actually exceed the amounts received as economic aid by foreign countries for the African continent (Fiano 2017).

This fact should not be overlooked by missionary candidates. That is why Ezemadu (2005) also mentions it as a source of funding. Dr. Sam George, from India, has served as a "catalyst for diasporas" for the Lausanne Committee; and in our personal discussions he recounted that these different groups of people are very generous in funding various projects related to world mission.

New advances in mobile banking make it easier to collect and send funds abroad. This is not a new funding model, but rather a new method of transferring funds from one account to another, and many people in the Majority World are already taking advantage of it. This allows people in the diaspora to send remittances to their home countries without difficulty. Mission agencies can take advantage of this new modality to communicate their financial needs, especially for projects and one-time needs, to Christians in the diaspora.

Chapter 6

Mission Funding 2.0

As we saw in the previous chapter, modifications can be applied to the traditional model to make it more effective. Nevertheless, criticism of this model continues to grow. Thus, other models should be considered. Some are well known and some are relatively unknown, but taken together they broaden the horizon for mission funding considerably. In the Majority World, it is time to move from Mission Funding 1.0 to Mission Funding 2.0.

Tentmakers

A model that a significant number of authors have been talking about for years is that of becoming a "tentmaker." This means that the missionary works on the mission field, earning a living through his or her own professional efforts. This model is clearly presented in Scripture (see Acts 18:3; 20:33–35; 1 Cor 4:12; 9:6; 1 Thess 2:6–9). Bjork argues that it was the normal practice of the Apostle Paul to meet his needs during his missionary travels and that "the funding of 'full-time' missionaries is, in fact, an historical anomaly" (Bjork 2015, 36).

Bjork maintains that it is wrong to think that mission is the business of local churches as institutions and that the faithful serve to support this apostolic work financially. For him, the church must return to the missionary model of the early church, based on the spread of the good news of Jesus by ordinary people. This is what he sometimes calls the intentional accompaniment of Christ's apprentices by other apprentices of Christ in their obedience to the Lord Jesus. Bjork believes that the church needs to give new value to lay missionaries in order to better understand the purpose and funding of mission and to move away from the idea of separate mission agencies.

I understand Bjork's concern. It would be wonderful to see the church doing much more, as he proposes, because more people would enter into a living relationship with the Lord. But that line of reasoning does not preclude other models of mission. As the Apostle Paul said, "I have become all things to all people so that *by all possible means* I might save some" (1 Cor 9:22; emphasis added).

I wouldn't say that there is no place for a mission agency in God's mission. Rather, I believe that in the "missionary model of the early church," of which Bjork speaks, there were people sent by a church, or churches, for cross-cultural mission. Otherwise, Paul wouldn't have asked the church in Rome to help him financially for his trip to Spain (Rom 15:24). Otherwise, Paul wouldn't have made so many missionary trips himself or argued that he had the right to receive financial assistance, even though he hadn't used that right himself (1 Cor 9:3–18). Or in the Old Testament, God wouldn't have sent Jonah to Nineveh to win over an enemy people (Jonah 1:1–2; 3:1–2) if some kind of apostolic work did not exist.

I believe there are places where "ordinary people" cannot go without a particular apostolic call. According to Paul, in Ephesians 4:11–13, some people, but not all, are called to be apostles; and some people, but not all, are called to be prophets; and some people, but not all, are called to be evangelists; and some people, but not all, are called to be pastors and teachers. There are many ways in which a believer can respond to an apostolic call, and being a "tentmaker" is one way of doing so, just as being sent out by a mission agency is another.

Several authors speak of this tentmaking model as an alternative to the traditional model (Pate 1989; Stevens 1999; Verwer 2000); and Craig Blomberg adds, regarding this bi-vocational model, that "in the Majority World it has been the norm for quite some time" (Blomberg 2013, 186). Evidence for this can be seen in the history of other missionary groups, such as the Moravians and those of the Basel Mission Trading Company (Danker 2002); the Batak missionaries from Indonesia around 1900 (Wong 1973); or, more recently, Nigerian missionaries sent by the Evangelical Missionary Society (Keyes 1983), Baptist missionaries from Malawi (Pate 1989), and Filipino women working in the Muslim world (Escobar 2003).

Others, such as Bessenecker (2014b) and Robinson (2014d), propose that this model should be used more for those serving in the parachurch white world. In other words, even in the Western world, where the traditional model was born, it is less and less effective, and other models should reinforce it. Moon (2013) agrees with this conclusion, saying that Korean missionaries need to make greater use of this tentmaking model to cope with costs and also to build relationships with people at the community level.

But some authors talk about both the advantages and disadvantages of becoming a tentmaker. Bessenecker notes that a great advantage is that this bi-vocational missionary model "embeds [God's] ministers into local institutions, connecting them more personally to the economies, services and cultures of a local community" (Bessenecker 2014a, loc. 1059). A good connection with the local population is exactly what a foreign missionary desires.

And it seems that a large number of countries will always be looking for competent people in certain fields, so this model should be valid for a long time to come. Dennis Clark (1971, 117) notes that we will see "a continuing flow of Christian technicians, agriculturalists, health and medical personnel, and consultants in every conceivable profession serving on long- or short-term assignments in Third World nations." The principle asserted in this remark is correct, even if in the meantime the areas of specialty have changed.

It should be added quickly that there are also serious drawbacks to tentmaking, and some authors talk about those as well. The most widespread problem seems to be that of making money. Of course, this applies especially to those who work on their own instead of working for a long-established company or organization.

An anonymous author writes in his unpublished dissertation, "Business as Mission: The Effective Use of Tentmaking in North Africa" (2011), that the biggest problem, according to his surveys, was the fact that only 17 percent of workers in North Africa had a business that made money. For this reason, the same author argues that the greatest need for tentmakers is to have "mentors" in business and commerce. But he adds that another need is "developing a kind of hybrid educational training for those whom God calls into a tentmaking ministry" ("Business as Mission," 138–39).

An education that brings theology and business together is indeed a very good idea for those who practice this model. Businesspeople in the evangelical church could surely benefit from such missiological training. But Patrick Lai (2005) warns that the language used by these two worlds is not the same and that communication must respect the values of both cultures.

Two other negative points have been raised by authors who deal with the topic of becoming a tentmaker. Clines (2006) believes that this model raises certain questions, such as how to be financially accountable to a leader. He suggests that this should happen more often than it does. The solution to this problem needs to be shared between tentmakers and their manager.

There is also the problem of having time to make disciples. Ronald Holcomb (1998) argues that tentmakers need to be seriously encouraged to make disciples and not just focus on the success of their business. In fact, quite often the business established by the tentmaker takes up so much time that he doesn't have sufficient time to devote to ministry, and thus he himself undermines the purpose of the business where he resides. This tension between having a business that makes money and having time to make disciples is indeed difficult for tentmakers to resolve.

This model is becoming more and more interesting as more and more countries are no longer admitting people as missionaries. So one must enter as a professional worker or as a worker in some trade. Preferably, a missionary should seek to occupy a position that local people aren't qualified for, such as a medical doctor, university teacher, or computer specialist, so as not to aggravate unemployment in the country or create jealousy. These tentmaking workers should be integrated into the mission agency as much as possible so that they don't live in loneliness as far as Christian fellowship is concerned, but this should be done in a very circumspect and discreet manner.

One obvious advantage of this model is that the missionary doesn't have to spend much time seeking financial support. It is true that his or her plane ticket will require seeking some extra funds, but apart from that these missionaries will provide for their financial needs themselves once they arrive on the mission field. This will allow them to arrive abroad fairly quickly without needing to worry about their salary, assuming that the work they have chosen is financially viable.

If the missionary has taken a professional job, which is ideal for this model, there will be far fewer financial problems compared to those who are looking to start their own business on the mission field. A professional job not only provides a sufficient salary but also a certain respect among the population, which is important for sharing the gospel. The advantages of this model are therefore numerous: it is biblical, it normally provides a sufficient financial salary, and it opens the door to relationships with the local population.

The tentmaking model is especially attractive to evangelical churches in the Majority World because missionaries don't have to seek their own financial support. According to my research, almost 50 percent of mission agencies in the Majority World use this model, which is both biblical and practical (Welch 2019). If a missionary can find professional work as an executive, this is an ideal way not only to receive adequate funding but also to have an open door to good relationships with the local population.

Sometimes, however, this model takes up too much time on the business side, not allowing enough time for the anticipated ministry. In addition, the literature suggests that too many practitioners of this model fail to develop a profitable business. I should note that many of the mission leaders in Ethiopia with whom I spoke consider the tentmaking model to be the preferred model for all missionary work in countries that are hostile to the gospel. Since these countries should be the focus of future missionary efforts, this tentmaking model will have its role to play there.

This model is certainly not without its difficulties. It is clear that the work done by the missionary can be time-consuming, leaving neither time nor energy to focus on the ministry that is often "on the side." How can you have a true ministry if the missionary is physically exhausted at the end of each day? In addition, despite all the time devoted to work, this model often doesn't provide enough income to live on. Third, another problem is that the missionary often sees his work as something separate from his ministry. This problem is best resolved with the business as mission (BAM) model. This model, which is the next one discussed, is an adaptation of the tentmaking model that has become increasingly common in many mission agencies, as it helps to address the problems faced by the tentmaker.

Business as Mission (BAM)

A model that is closely related to the previous one, but is nevertheless different, is the "business as mission" model—or BAM for short. The biggest difference between a tentmaking missionary and a BAM missionary is that the former seeks a job that already exists or creates a small job for himself or herself, while the latter seeks to create a small business that hires other people. In other words, a tentmaking missionary can be seen as someone who takes a job from a local person, while a BAM missionary is someone who creates a job for a local person (Swanson 2010).

Thomas Sudyk says that BAM is more readily accepted by host cultures than the traditional model (Yamamori and Eldred 2003), thus opening the door to "restricted countries," in terms of mission. This is consistent with the ideas of Steffen and Barnett (2006), who say that BAM holds great promise on a global scale. Mordomo (Steffen and Barnett 2006) maintains that BAM is biblical, practical, and effective. Clark was far ahead of his peers when he asked, "Why should Christians of the [Majority World] continue to remain as employees instead of senior partners and shareholders in a consortium?" (Clark 1971, 109). BAM seeks to produce such results.

The BAM model resembles the tentmaking model, except that BAM places more emphasis on business start-ups and job creation than does tentmaking. This model is interesting, because even countries hostile to the gospel want their economies to succeed. Such businesspeople/entrepreneurs should therefore be integrated into a mission agency so that they are not alone on the one hand, and so they can be accountable to a corporate spiritual body on the other. And before sending such a missionary/entrepreneur abroad, the businessmen in the sending country could play an important role in the training of these missionary "workers," integrating them more into the missionary program of the church.

An advantage of this model is that it is often more holistic than the tentmaking model, since the BAM practitioner sees his or her work and employees as the primary focus, and not as something on the outside, of his or her ministry. Such a model is uni-vocational instead of bi-vocational. Like authors who support the idea of the theology of work (Stevens 1999; Mtata 2011; Keller 2014), the BAM missionary sees work as an integral part of his or her ministry—and it does not create a false dichotomy between the sacred and the secular. When done well, this model provides a good salary not only to the missionary/worker, but also to local people in the community.

Not everything concerning BAM, however, is positive. One disadvantage is that it requires a large amount of capital before starting, which is higher than the simple financial support of a missionary and therefore harder to raise. Second, setting up a business in a foreign culture where business practices are different from those in one's home country is not at all easy. As a result, the success rate for BAM missionaries is often not very high.

Steffen and Barnett (2006) also discuss some of the negative aspects of BAM, including the idea that the model is based on American values and ideology, and that some BAM practitioners see capitalism as God's strategy for evangelizing the world. At times the zeal of BAM practitioners seems to override their common sense!

SIM's experience with business as mission in Asia is that practitioners need much more business training; their enthusiasm exceeds their practical knowledge (Welch 2019). This is consistent with what the anonymous author from North Africa (2011) said: There is a great need for mentors for missionaries who want to start a small business.

Business as mission is a very good idea, but the execution of that idea can be difficult. Another practical problem is that of personal relationships between missionaries. Regarding those who choose this new model, Lai says that "the scope of their assignment creates problems and stresses which are unique and different from those experienced by regular missionaries. ... [They] find they are unable to relate to one another" (Lai 2005, loc. 200).

While relational problems exist within the BAM model, and sometimes practitioners rely too much on funding from the West, the next model is also facing some of these same difficulties. I am talking about the model of establishing partnerships between churches and Christian organizations.

Partnerships

Another model that many writers and researchers address is partnerships. This model, at least initially, came from Western churches and Christian organizations that regularly contributed to churches or organizations in the Majority World. It was assumed that churches and ministries in the Majority World needed this Western funding (see Bush 1990; Taylor 1994), although these authors emphasized the idea of interdependent partnerships. The Western share was almost always the financial share. Later, Escobar refers to this same idea, more or less, by calling this "the cooperative method" (Escobar 2003, 67).

Interestingly, Clark (1971, 48) also discussed this idea of cooperation between churches and ministries around the world, but he recognized from the beginning that this model should not be used for local church work in the mission field:

> Finances for local church work can be supplied in nearly all cases by local people, according to their standards of income and expenditure. The introduction of foreign funds for church work has a debilitating effect and weakens local initiative.

This warning underlies the criticisms of this model. Robertson McQuilkin (1999) explains five negative points of this model if the partnership becomes solely a relationship where money comes from the Western partner:

1. Believers depend neither on God nor on themselves, but on the donors.
2. Leaders become preoccupied with North American funds.
3. Many lawsuits arise between believers over land purchased by these funds.
4. An "aristocracy" is created among the servants of God—between those who are "connected" and those who are not.
5. Those who receive these funds end up becoming ungrateful.

Fred Wilson (1994) sought to avoid these problems by offering to send personnel in addition to money, but he had to admit that if his church sent someone to the mission field, the Western partner made the decisions and the local partner withdrew from the partnership. Partnerships can work well, but they are much harder to achieve if one partner's only asset is money.

Mary Lederleitner (2010) summarizes well by saying that relationships based on trust, respect, mutual dignity, good communication, and humility have the best chance of forming a good partnership, and this is especially true when dealing with the question of how to use funds to finance a ministry. Lederleitner's book, *Cross-Cultural Partnerships: Navigating the Complexities of Money and Mission*, considers on the one hand the importance of trusting relationships between partners, and on the other hand recognizing the Majority World partner as an equal partner. These essential truths need to be put into practice if a partnership has any hope of remaining healthy.

After looking at the most common models, we can also consider some models that are less well known but could be very useful in the Majority World. The modest literature that exists deals with these other models in the North American context; virtually no literature presents these options in the Majority World context.

Seeking Support from the Mission, Not the Missionary

In this model the mission agency, and especially its president or general director, seeks financial support for its missionaries. According to my research, this model is widely used in India, as all five mission agencies I contacted used this model (Welch 2019). As already mentioned, this model is very useful in countries where it is not culturally acceptable for a person to ask for financial support for themselves.

The advantage of this model is that usually the president/director of a mission agency is more capable and experienced in seeking financial support than is an inexperienced, brand-new missionary. Moreover, this missionary leader is usually widely known to church leaders and can more easily obtain a speaking engagement at local churches.

There are, however, disadvantages to this model. The fact that the entire mission agency's financial approach depends on a single person or a very small number of leaders means that fundraising is based on a rather precarious foundation. If the president/director falls ill for a period of time, all of that agency's missionaries suffer the consequences, with their salaries declining because of their director's illness. In the same vein, if a new director is less dynamic than his predecessor, the whole mission must bear the consequences, possibly for a long period of time.

The model where mission leaders—not the missionaries themselves—seek missionary funding is a fairly promising model for the Majority World. According to my research, 50 percent of the world's major non-Western mission agencies already use this model, perhaps because their leaders have more "connections" with local churches and more experience in fundraising. As long as these leaders are good at doing their job and stay healthy, this model works well, according to my findings from both India and Africa.

In SIM's Northeast India office, they use a hybrid of this model. While they ask missionaries to raise support to cover their salary and ministry activities, the mission seeks to raise the money for all of the administrative expenses related to sending a missionary family to the field. That includes expenses such as health insurance, retirement pension, administrative fees that go to both the field and sending office, taxes, etc. Mission office personnel seek to raise these funds, as they are the expenses that are less directly related to the ministry being performed. While those expenses are indeed legitimate, local churches have a more difficult time with sending money to cover them. So the mission, and not the missionary, seeks to cover those costs for those SIM missionaries from Northeast India

Twelve-Church Model

With this model, local churches initiate the raising of financial support for missionary families. One local church partners with eleven other local churches, and each month one of these twelve churches will provide the monthly support for a missionary family based on the month it has chosen. In this way, a church will send funds to a missionary the first time for its designated month and then have a full year to raise the funds the second time around. Upon their return, the missionary family will visit "their" twelve churches.

A church in Guayaramerin, Bolivia, and its pastor, Christian Rocha, used a similar model to send a missionary family to Equatorial Guinea. With this model it is not necessary for all twelve churches to be in the same denomination, although if that is the case, it may facilitate some of the logistical aspects of fundraising.

A similar example from Peru involves the Christian and Missionary Alliance Church. However, instead of each of the twelve churches providing one month of financial support, the home church provides 40 percent of the financial support and the other eleven churches provide the remaining 60 percent. Several missionaries are receiving financial support from this group of twelve churches. Each year the twelve churches hold a large missions congress, with speakers who travel from church to church. This allows for new ideas and motivations for missions to percolate among these churches.

Three passages could serve as the biblical basis for this model, in that they show a monthly rotation of responsibility or production for twelve months. We see this with the leadership of David's army (1 Chr 27:1–15), the administration of Solomon's kingdom (1 Kgs 4:7–19), and the tree of life in paradise (Rev 22:2).

This model has the advantage of being very simple to understand, and it also has the advantage of giving a whole year to get the same amount of financial support the second time around. In addition, if a church finds that it is no longer able to participate in the fundraising program, it can look for another church in the same denomination to replace it.

This model could work fairly easily in a denomination that has a large number of local churches in one country or region. An advantage for the missionary family is that it has twelve churches to visit during their home assignment, which gives them the opportunity to get to know a large number of families on a personal level and can provide even more prayer and financial support.

A disadvantage of this model is that it may be difficult for a family to visit twelve churches if their home assignment is only a few months long. A second difficulty is encountered when a local church does not send its money on time, or if it decides to withdraw its financial support of the designated missionary in the middle of his or her stay abroad. In such a case the missionary family could face some serious financial difficulties on the field, being obliged to spend a lot of time themselves trying to find a church to take over the negligent church's pledged support.

The "twelve-church model" seems to be practical for evangelical churches in the Majority World because it is simple to implement administratively and not too tiring for the missionary family upon returning from the field, at least if the twelve churches are in the same part of the country. This promising model needs to be tried much more to see if it brings in the desired results, and it seems like it could also work well in the Western world where a greater number of large denominations exist.

"Revolving Savings" for Mission

Another model where the local church initiates missionary funding is called a "revolving savings" plan. Under this model, each week a certain amount of money—either a percentage or a lump sum—is taken out of the general offering and put into the mission "cash box." Thus, at the end of the month, assuming that the church supports twelve missionaries, one missionary can benefit from it each month.

If the church decides to support six missionaries instead of twelve, the church can send its support bi-monthly. For example, if a church decides to support each of six missionary families at $100/month, it can set aside $150 every week from the offering and put it in the mission cash box. At the end of the month, the church will have $600 to send to these six families. Or, at the end of two months, it will have $1200 to send, or $200 to each of these six missionary families (2 x $100/month = $200).

This model is based on a practice that already exists in many churches in the Majority World, but usually not for mission funding. Often it is the women's group, or the youth group, or another group in the church that uses this model. By using this model that combines a cultural practice with a need in the local church, the amount of the budget line for mission or for missionary families will already be provided.

A variation of this model could be used by a group of local churches instead of a single church. Six churches, for example, could contribute each month to the savings plan for a specific missionary family, and every two months one of them funds that family. Perhaps other variations of this model could be tried. For example, the mission start-up group (MSG) could oversee such a revolving savings plan within the local church.

In a sense, this model remains hypothetical, because so far I have not personally been able to study or investigate the churches that use it for mission funding, even though other groups in the church use it primarily as a personal savings account for their members. Some groups designate a certain percentage of the funds to go to the church budget, but most do not.

The use of a revolving savings plan for raising funds for mission could be very beneficial, as it is a practice that is well known and already used in hundreds of churches in the Majority World. A group of evangelical churches could come together to fund a small group of missionaries. It would be interesting to see how applicable this model is to mission funding.

In addition, there are no exorbitant fees associated with this method compared to the cost of bookkeeping and other bank charges. Three churches/ missions in Ethiopia have reported that they are already using this method for mission (Welch 2019). In spite of the fact that a more extensive study of their results has yet to be done, I believe that this method will quickly spread to other parts of the world.

Crowdfunding

Linked to the previous model is what is technically called *participatory financing*, although it is more commonly known by the term *crowdfunding*. Elimane Sembène calls the revolving savings plans mentioned above "the financial umbrellas that are the true ancestors and probable sources of inspiration for modern crowdfunding" (Sembène 2015, 58). A practitioner in the field of participatory finance, Thierry Barbaut, says that "crowdfunding is perfectly suited to Africa" (Sembène 2015, 51).

This method of fundraising is done by publishing financial needs on a website such as GoFundMe or Kickstarter, and then the general public can decide whether or not to contribute. This model is more appealing to young people because they are more used to contributing through electronic means. In Kenya, there is already a service called M-Changa, which offers "an application that operates through easy and free registration and transparent tracking arrangements that allow clients to raise funds via their cell phones" (Sembène 2015, 52). A mission agency could create its own "platform" for crowdfunding and thus finance construction or development projects, as this model is more effective for tangible objectives than for intangible ones, such as monthly financial support for a missionary.

Crowdfunding has the advantage of being able to quickly make financial needs known to a very large audience, given the fact that 4,260,117,793 people (84.2 percent of all internet users) live in the Majority World, compared to 1,125,680,613 people (15.8 percent of all internet users) who live in the Western world (Miniwatts Marketing Group 2022).

However, this model is problematic. Even if a large number of people can access the internet, it is difficult for them to make a bank transaction through this means, since in Africa and elsewhere there is a "low rate of banking … [and] many African countries still prohibit payments by credit card" (Sembène 2015, 52). In addition, many countries in the Majority World lack the necessary infrastructure to ensure an efficient internet. These impediments risk obstructing effective crowdfunding until solutions are found, hopefully in the near future.

At the same time, certain mission agencies do not permit crowdfunding, even for its more tangible project needs. Instead, they offer a similar service with anonymous giving on their own websites. And in my own limited experience with those mission agencies that do allow crowdfunding for projects, they have had only limited success. But that doesn't mean that this model will not be more effective in the future.

Living Off the Fruit of Ministry

This funding model is often used secondarily—that is, another model is used at the beginning of a ministry to meet daily needs, and then once the ministry has been well established on the mission field, the missionary adopts this additional model to meet his or her financial expenses.

This model is most effective for a church-planting ministry, because the normal continuation of church planting is the spiritual maturity of new believers, and this includes generosity to God for the continuation of the ministry. For example, a missionary does evangelism on the mission field, and after a period of time begins a Sunday service in the home of one of the new converts. During this time the missionary lives off the financial support that he has had to seek himself and which is sent to him by his mission agency each month. But after five years those who participate in the Sunday service number forty people, including about twenty people who are employed. Each worshiper is encouraged to participate in church offerings, and over time these people become more generous, as many offer tithes from their salaries.

In this way the missionary no longer needs the support he received from abroad, because those who represent the fruit of his ministry contribute enough themselves to support him 100 percent. So he stops the financial support that came through the earlier model of raising his own support and adopts this new model of living off the fruit of his ministry.

This model is quite widespread in the Majority World, as a large number of pastors use it, including those who preach the "prosperity gospel," where this model seems to be the most popular. It should be added that this model also works for other areas or ministry projects, such as launching a radio station or a publishing house. If a revenue component is normally part of the ministry project, that project can adopt this model at the appropriate time.

One difficulty with this model is that the missionary may sometimes live off the fruit of his ministry for a time, but the economic situation of the city or region may change, and eventually the people in his ministry are no longer able to support him.

Many missionaries in the area of church planting live off the "spiritual fruit" of their ministry. This model works quite well in the Majority World, because new Christians in these parts of the world are generally very grateful for their new life in Christ and consequently are very generous toward their new church. Calvary Ministries in Nigeria, along with the Agence Missionnaire Interafricaine, its French-speaking branch in Côte d'Ivoire, as well as churches in Ethiopia, confirm this generosity. This is a model that should continue to be used.

Support That Diminishes over Time

Another model, a modification of the previous one, is one in which financial support decreases over time. Here either the missionary, the mission agency, or the church can initiate the search for funds, but after a certain time the amount received by the missionary begins to gradually decrease. Calvary Ministries in Nigeria uses this model, where the fruit of the ministry increasingly covers the financial support of the missionary. For example, a missionary is supported 100 percent in the first year by the mission agency or church that sent him or her, 80 percent in the second year, 60 percent in the third year, and so on until the newly planted church has the means to cover 100 percent of the missionary's expenses. At that time the church may replace the missionary with a pastor, and the missionary is free to begin another church-planting ministry elsewhere. The Apostle Paul indirectly spoke of this model; see, for example, 1 Corinthians 9:3–8 and Galatians 6:6.

The time to finally discontinue financial support may differ depending on the circumstances of the ministry. One disadvantage often occurs when the mission agency sets a time in advance to stop missionary funding, but at that point the ministry still cannot adequately support the missionary.

Decreasing financial support over time is a practical model for the Majority World, as it allows missionaries to stop seeking mission funding after a period of time, which is the goal of many missionaries. But the difficulty will be knowing by how much to decrease financial support. In addition, the right time to end financial support from outside may take longer than expected, making this model a bit complicated to master. One must take into account local circumstances and not make a rule that applies to all countries in the Majority World regarding these aspects of this model.

A "Handful of Rice" (*buhfai tham*)

This model is interesting for two reasons: first, because it comes from the Majority World, and second, because it has been practiced for more than a hundred years. In northeast India, the women of the church set aside a single handful of rice (*buhfai tham*) at each meal. They regularly bring the rice to the church, and the local church sells the rice and uses the proceeds for mission. When the program began in 1910, this money was used to send women evangelists to a certain region. They were called "Bible women," according to the Global Generosity Movement (2010).

It is obvious that in other parts of the world the handful of rice could be a handful of millet or corn, a piece of charcoal, a bundle of wood, and so on. In 2010 alone, this program provided mission funding worth the equivalent of 1.5 million US dollars (Global Generosity Movement 2010). The Presbyterian Church of Mizoram sends and supports more than 1,800 missionaries using this model, and it should not be forgotten that the state of Mizoram remains one of the poorest states in the whole country of India.

This model is also interesting because it shows that people who care about mission, even if they are financially limited, can accomplish a lot for the Lord. A missionary leader in Ethiopia reported that his church denomination uses this model in the south of the country, a part of the country that is quite poor (Welch 2019). This model holds great promise for the Majority World. It demonstrates that vision is more important than economics in mission financing, and the Western church would do well to take a page out of the Majority World church's playbook.

The "handful of rice" model has already shown that it is feasible in the Majority World, especially in India but also in Ethiopia, according to my research. One great advantage of this model is that it allows even the poorest people to participate in global mission. Many local churches should try it by exchanging rice with the seeds or food of their choice.

Chris Conti, a mission mobilizer in South America with SIM, reported that this model has been a great resource to help people understand that every little bit helps. It has been exciting for her to see people understand that they can offer whatever is locally available in their community. Some churches have collected and sold eggs. A few churches have held parades in rural areas, with those participating then giving their first livestock or their first basket of fruit or vegetables for mission.

Part-Time Employment for Spouse

Sometimes a spouse may find a job that opens the door to a new area of ministry. We know that Priscilla worked alongside her husband Aquila in tentmaking (see Acts 18:3), and that this pattern can be replicated. Today, for example, one can teach conversation classes in the missionary's mother tongue, or offer English classes or computer classes. Many people would like to know how to master their computers, such as how to better use word-processing software or spreadsheets. Or a spouse may be able to play a musical instrument and give music lessons to the children in the church or neighborhood.

The basic idea here is to turn a particular skill into a part-time job. If there is enough demand for this kind of work, it could even become a "tentmaking" job, eliminating the need for an alternative funding model in the long run. At the same time, having a part-time job makes it easier for the "worker" to explain to others why he or she is in that foreign country.

The disadvantage of this model is that the part-time work can greatly distract missionaries from their primary ministry and focus their attention on financial and non-spiritual outcomes. But if the missionary is disciplined, he or she can control the situation fairly easily and not allow the work to take up too much of their time.

Part-time employment by a spouse is sometimes possible in the Majority World, especially if the person has talents that are sought after by the local population and the "job" can be done at home. This model is less successful if a wife has to seek employment in a store or in the civil service, since some countries in the Majority World do not easily accept women in the workplace. However, I know of a number of missionary wives who worked for years in Cote d'Ivoire as teachers in an international school or as a nurse in an embassy. Such employment not only brought in extra income, but also allowed for ministry opportunities among students or patients.

Reducing Costs

This model is the opposite of all the others in the sense that one should not only seek to increase revenues for mission funding but should also seek to reduce costs. For example, seven men from a local church, even if they don't have a job, can support a mission agency by serving once a week as volunteer night watchmen, volunteer maintenance workers, etc. This shows that an unemployed person can, even without money, support mission.

Or the local church can mobilize its members to care for missionary families when they return on home assignment. For example, a doctor who is a member of the church could provide free or discounted medical checkups for a missionary family; a real estate agent who is a member of the church could help them find housing at a discounted price; church members could lend furniture to the missionary family while they are home from overseas; someone from the church could offer the family a weekend getaway at a hotel where they can rest; a school principal could admit missionary children at a reduced price when they are back for their home assignment; a family with two vehicles could offer one to the missionary family while they are back in their home country; farmers could offer a small portion of their harvest to a missionary family, etc.

Similarly, an accountant could volunteer to do the annual financial statements and taxes for a mission agency; five people could volunteer to be a receptionist one day a week; painters, plumbers, and carpenters could offer their services on an ad hoc basis, etc. All these gestures help reduce costs for a missionary family or a mission agency. According to my research, mission agencies in India, Thailand, South Africa, Ethiopia, Kenya, Nigeria, Austria, Romania, and Ecuador reduce their costs by using volunteers, showing that this model is already quite widespread in the Majority World (Welch 2019).

Cost reduction by mission agencies is a model that is easily applied in the Majority World, as these agencies are constantly seeking such reductions. My research has shown that a majority of these agencies (77 percent) often use volunteer staff and that their staff often use public transportation (71 percent), both of which are ways of putting this model into practice. The vast majority of their missionary staff (90 percent) choose a simple lifestyle. At the same time, simplification of administrative procedures will always be welcome in the Majority World, as elsewhere. Progress in banking, information, and telephone systems allows for this simplification and the accompanying reduction in costs.

Endowment Fund

When a mission agency decides to open an endowment fund, it is also deciding not to touch the fund principal for the agency's current needs. Rather, such a fund earns long-term interest, and this interest can be used to meet the operational costs of the mission or of a specific project. The board of directors of a mission agency might decide that a certain percentage of all donations above a certain amount will be put into such a fund. In this way, the agency begins to create a fund for future use. Of course, one must be wise in investing and avoid funds with a supposedly "guaranteed" high rate of return. Sufficient research must be conducted prior to investing money.

But from time to time a mission agency receives the bequest of a large donation, and instead of spending it all at once, it would be wiser to devote part or all of it to an endowment fund. Some Western mission agencies manage to generate more than one thousand US dollars per month in bank interest alone, and generally interest rates are higher in the Majority World than in the Western world.

The essential principles of such a fund are that 1) mission leaders think today about how to generate funds for the future, and 2) that these same leaders resist dipping into the fund principal for current needs. A disadvantage of this model is that missionaries who are aware of such a fund may no longer trust God for their funding. Instead, they may rely on the economic market, which would have other negative consequences for their ministry.

Supporting a Ministry instead of a Missionary Person/Family

After a sufficient time of prayer and research, a church may decide to support a specific ministry (literature, radio, Bible translation, youth ministry, or evangelism among a specific unreached people group—e.g., Tuareg, Wolof, Fulani, Turkmen, Uyghur, Uzbek) instead of supporting a specific missionary. That church can also decide how much it wants to contribute each year and set this as an annual goal for mission. Thereafter it could contribute to a specific mission agency that is working in the desired ministry, or to a missionary who serves in the chosen ministry or with the chosen people.

The specific idea here is that one is supporting a *type* of ministry instead of a particular person. This model is advantageous for a local church that does not personally know missionaries who are involved in a ministry of choice. It is also a good funding model for a time-limited project, because from the beginning the local church knows the deadline for its financial commitment.

Supporting a ministry instead of a missionary allows evangelical churches in the Majority World to choose a project or ministry that they can support for a period of time. This model is advantageous because it doesn't extend indefinitely, as is often the case when supporting a missionary family. Some ministries and almost all projects have a deadline for their completion, which makes this model more attractive to local churches.

"Mission Designation"

With this model, individual members of a local church initiate mission funding. Church members who are farmers, for example, may designate a certain portion of their land for mission. Or members who are herders may designate one cow or two sheep or three goats as animals for mission when they are butchered. Or a farmer who raises chickens, rabbits, etc. may designate every fifteenth or twentieth animal sold for mission. When they are sold, the profits go to missionary families or to a mission agency.

Another possibility is that those in the church who are merchants and salespeople may designate the profits from sales on a certain day of the month as "missionary profits." The advantage of this model is its flexibility: you can designate the sale of an animal for mission; you can designate a piece of land for mission; you can designate a day of the month, an hour of the day, a morning of the week, a vehicle in a fleet, a chair or table in a restaurant, every n^{th} customer, etc. The possibilities are endless.

According to the director of the mission SIM in Australia, a farmer in Papua New Guinea named a cow "India," and when the cow was sold, the profit was designated for a mission agency working in India. He also recounts that a farmer had designated a certain parcel of his land for mission, knowing that it was not a good piece of land. To his astonishment, God blessed that parcel with the best harvest of all his land. Not only was the mission blessed, but the farmer also grew in his faith. According to my research in Ethiopia, in one church some banana farmers designated three banana trees for the mission. In another church, farmers regularly donate a sheep or goat for mission (Welch 2019).

The "mission designation" model comes from the Majority World. Like the "handful of rice" model, it allows relatively poor people to participate in global mission by designating a good or a service, setting them apart for general funding. With more awareness, this model could positively impact a large number of evangelical churches that want to engage in global mission. It would be an excellent model to put into practice in the Western church as well.

Simplified Procedures

Linked to the reduction of costs, mission agencies also need to simplify administrative procedures as much as possible. For example, agencies could charge a monthly flat fee as an administrative fee for processing their missionaries' gift income, tax payments, etc., instead of setting a percentage of the monthly revenue to be taken. This avoids the need to occupy the time of an accountant to calculate all the income of each missionary.

Another example is giving donors the opportunity to contribute directly to missionaries through a cell phone or mobile money account (M-Pesa, Orange Money, MoMo, etc.) instead of sending their money directly to the mission agency. This removes the need for regular bank transfers and reduces a mission agency's bank charges at the same time. Alternatively, a mission agency can give each missionary a credit (or debit) card, and its missionaries can make withdrawals at ATMs in their city.

Such opportunities exist more and more in the Majority World. This principle is very useful for the missionary who prefers not to spend too much time on administrative work and also for donors who are reluctant to contribute to the administration of the mission, even though they admit that this administrative aspect is unavoidable.

Mission Agencies That Contribute to the Local Church

Another model for a mission agency is to contribute to the life of local churches. One reason for such a model is that too often mission agencies are perceived as stealing people and money from the church. They are seen as those who take—not those who give. So mission agencies should also give back to the church by presenting seminars, for example, on unreached peoples, the persecuted church, BAM opportunities, prayer for mission, etc. They can help local churches with the formation of mission start-up groups (MSGs) or educate on how to develop a mission strategy. They could even contribute financially each year to the ministry of a local church chosen by their board of directors.

This willingness to contribute to churches, instead of always asking churches to contribute to the mission agency, can mobilize a spirit of collaboration between the two entities, which may result in the long run in a better missionary vision for the church and more funding for mission.

Like their Western counterparts, Majority World mission agencies need to consider how they can contribute to the growth of the local church in relation to mission. They also need to adopt a mentality of giving to the local church and not just receiving from the local church. Such a mentality contributes to the partnership between mission agencies and evangelical churches—a partnership that exemplifies the heart of global mission.

Activities and Events

Finally, the local church may initiate events and activities to promote both mission and missionary vision, as well as to generate income for mission. With a little thought and creativity, this list could be much longer. Here are a number of ideas from my own research and experience:

1) A church could hold a "mission week" each year, in which the church's offering is designated for mission. During the week, activities (such as movies, concerts, sports, a "national meal," seminars, etc.) could take place at the church, and the proceeds from ticket sales for some of these activities could also go toward mission.

2) A church could designate a project that generates income as its missionary project. For example, the church could purchase a vehicle, such as a taxicab, and give the profits from it to one or two missionary families. Or the church could purchase two dairy cows and sell the milk produced. The proceeds will support a mission agency chosen by the church. Or the church could build apartments or offices and then use the rental income to finance the ministry. These ideas are interesting, but so far there is little documentation on the effectiveness of such efforts.

3) A church could host artists from the local church (painters, wood-carvers, photographers, potters, etc.) and have an exhibit that showcases their talents. Afterward an auction, open to the public, could be held, with the proceeds going toward mission. A church in England did this in 2012 during a "national week" (like the national week of the woman, or the national week of the child). Such an activity not only earns money for mission, but it shows local community leaders that the church is interested in what they are doing.

4) A church could organize a "concert for missions," with musicians, singers, dancers, and poets. The proceeds would go to a pre-defined need, such as mission in "closed" countries, how to help the poor, how to defend street children and orphans, etc. Since a single local church is unlikely to have enough participants, this event could be opened to churches in the whole denomination. After the sale of tickets, any profit goes to support the missionaries working in the given ministry. This same idea could be adapted by showing documentary films, instead of hosting a concert, that deal with a certain topic.

5) A church could organize a training seminar for missionaries and businesspeople. Businessmen and businesswomen will help missionaries in certain areas, such as computer skills (how to better use word-processing software, or Excel, or some notions of accounting, or taxes, etc.). Missionaries will help businesspeople to better share the gospel or show them how businesspeople or "political" people in the Bible (Abraham, Nehemiah, Daniel, etc.) advanced the kingdom of God. By doing so, missionaries do not necessarily receive financial support, but they do receive business training, and businesspeople are given mission knowledge and opportunities.

6) A similar idea is for a local church to train people for a profession (hairdresser, urban agriculture, computer consultant, car repair, teaching English or French, etc.) and then send these trained people as "tentmaking" missionaries. The church will support them in prayer and upon their return from the mission field, but it will not be required to provide all of the missionary's salary, but only part of it. A mission in Ethiopia does this kind of

training and sends people to countries that do not formally accept someone as a missionary. Another mission in Ethiopia trained someone to dig a well. He then managed the well and sold water to the community.

7) A church could organize a soccer game where the youth play against the pastors and missionaries. The church launches a campaign beforehand in which the members promise to give so much money for every goal scored by the youth or the pastors/missionaries. If the pastors/missionaries win, 60 percent of the money goes to the mission and 40 percent goes to the youth program. If the youth win, the youth group receives 60 percent of the funds. Or, alternately, you don't have a soccer game but a penalty shootout, and people promise so much money for every goal scored by the pastors/missionaries or the youth. Again, the team that wins receives 60 percent of the funds raised and the team that loses receives 40 percent. (The church can choose any percentage it wants; these percentages are simply suggestions.)

8) A mission agency could organize "exotic evenings," in which the missionaries prepare a typical dinner from the mission field where they serve—with typical music, typical clothing, a history of the country, etc. This evening serves to inform the church members about mission, and the missionary concerned receives the profits from the sale of tickets to attend the evening.

9) Christian authors could contribute by donating part of their royalties to the mission or bringing all the royalties from a specific book to support a missionary family. A missionary family in Côte d'Ivoire benefited from the royalty payments of an author friend for one of his books. Christian artists can do the same thing with their albums or dedicate one out of ten concerts to mission.

10) A church could organize a "mission quiz show" between the youth and the adults as a kind of initiation to mission. Church members purchase an inexpensive ticket to watch the show. That way, the youth of the church learn more about mission, as do the church members, and a mission agency or family receives the profit from the sale of the tickets.

11) A church could organize a bicycle race, a 5K or 10K run, etc. for its members. People promise so much money for every kilometer they run/walk/ride, and the proceeds go to mission. It is also very good for the health of the participants. You could do the same thing with basketball teams, or a "free throw" contest, with a sum of money promised for each successful free throw.

12) The youth of the church could take water and soap, and one Saturday afternoon each month they could wash the vehicles belonging to church members or neighbors. Half of the money collected will be given to a

mission agency and the other half will be kept for the youth group. Or, as a youth group in Ethiopia did, they stand at the entrance of the church with shoeshine polish and clean the shoes of those who come in (if they agree). These "clients" make a contribution and the money is given to support mission. The principle here is that the youth are doing a service to the church members and the money received goes toward mission.

13) A church could organize a play and the church members could be the actors. The proceeds from the sale of tickets will be given to a mission agency or allocated for the support of a missionary family.

14) A few Christian herders/farmers could get together and send a cow, a goat, fruit, vegetables, yams, rice, etc. to a mission agency. All this food could be prepared by church members and then frozen and used for several months during mission orientation classes, training courses, etc. There are churches in the US that do this every year, and it helps reduce the costs of the mission agency.

15) If the church has a piece of property, it could grow what it wants and allocate the proceeds for mission. Or if it has a building with an empty office, it could rent the office to someone else and the income could be used for mission. The idea here is that one can use what already exists for mission. A mission agency in Côte d'Ivoire had a building with six apartments in it, and the rent from the six apartments went toward the operating costs of the ministry.

16) A church in Ethiopia bought hundreds of pens, had a Bible verse printed on them, and then sold them for double the purchase price. Some church members paid more than double. The profit from the sale went for mission.

17) A church may make small wooden boxes and distribute them to church members. At home, a family that is enthusiastic about mission can regularly put money into the box, and on a given Sunday all the families who participate in this contest bring their boxes to the church. There the boxes are opened, and the money collected goes for mission, with prizes (books, Bibles, etc.) for those who contribute the largest amounts. One church denomination in Ethiopia used this practice to generate funds for mission with great success.

18) Members of a church's mission start-up group (MSG) could organize the sale of Christmas items, cookies, yogurt, etc., and the proceeds go toward mission. They could make small bracelets with the name of a country, a family, an unreached people group, or something else written on it. The bracelets serve as a reminder to pray for the country or people group connected with it.

———————

All of these models, like all of the events and activities mentioned above, serve to expand our idea of what a church, mission agency, or missionary can do to meet the financial support required to go abroad for global mission. All of these models are suitable for missionary work in the Majority World and can be adapted to suit the situation. If only more evangelical churches were aware of these various models instead of focusing solely on the traditional model, I believe that these churches could more easily engage in global mission. And these models already being used by churches in the Majority World can also be implemented by churches in the Western world, demonstrating a kind of give-and-take in terms of learning from one another.

Benefits of Mission Funding 2.0

Global mission is first and foremost God's ministry. God is the author of mission; he is the one who seeks to win back his own creatures who have rejected him, and his seeking affects all the people on this planet. From the creation of humans until the return of Jesus, God has sought, is seeking, and will always seek people who recognize him as the one Lord God of all the earth and of all nations.

From Genesis to Revelation, God reveals himself as a missionary God.[1] Regarding this mission of God, Glenn Smith (2005, 51) notes:

> The *missio Dei* establishes the priority of God's missionary activity and characterizes God as a God who is himself missionary in nature. In this case, mission cannot be understood as primarily a church activity or program. It must flow from God Himself.

This is how the church of God collaborates with what God is already doing in the world. Mission is not just a church program, as Smith says; it is the church's *raison d'être*. Or to put it another way, it's not so much that the people of God have a mission as it is that the mission of God has a people. This has been true from Genesis 1. This explains why the church must take global mission seriously. Since missionary activity is God's priority, the church needs to give serious thought to funding this priority.

In light of that strategic point, one benefit resulting from this research is to identify a number of these new models of mission funding, what I call Mission Funding 2.0, and decide which ones will be best suited to your situation in the Majority World. These models will enlighten those who want to participate in mission but don't know how to do so. By proposing these other models, evangelical churches in Africa, Asia, Eastern Europe, and Latin America will know that other funding models exist and are more appropriate to their situation. As a result, these new mission funding models will allow for more missionaries to be sent around the world, since it will be less difficult for them to find financial resources.[2]

---

[1] Starting at Genesis 1:28, the first verse in the Bible in which God speaks to the first human beings, God explains that his plan of action is for the whole earth, because the man and his wife are commanded to fill the earth. Often this order is interpreted as a kind of "cultural mandate," but the spiritual element should not be overlooked. If the spiritual element was not paramount, God would *not* have condemned all those people in Genesis 6 who were actually filling the earth. But God wants a people who obey him as members of his family. Later, God repeated this same command to Noah and his sons, telling them to fill the earth (Gen 9:1). Later, he told Abraham that "all peoples on earth will be blessed through you" (Gen 12:3).

This kind of universal *missio Dei* can be seen in other passages, such as Joshua 4:24, 1 Kings 8:60, Psalms 2:8 and 96:3, Isaiah 49:6, Matthew 28:19–20, Luke 24:46–47, and Acts 1:8. And God will remain a missionary God in the future. Revelation 5:6 speaks of "the seven spirits of God sent out into all the earth." Three verses later (5:9) we see the worship of God coming from people "from every tribe and language and people and nation." Then, in Revelation 21:24, we see that "the nations will walk by [the Lamb's] light, and the kings of the earth will bring their splendor into it." Also, there will be a tree of life whose leaves "are for the healing of the nations" (22:2). From beginning to end, God has a heart for all the nations and all the peoples of the earth. He is and will remain a missionary God.

[2] This assumes that the church will always have a heart for mission, as it does today, and that it will always seek to be seriously involved in global mission.

This growth in the mission work force will pertain not only to the Majority World, which will utilize models from both Mission Funding 1.0 and 2.0, but it can pertain equally to the Western world which should also experiment with these new approaches. Models of seeking financial support that are better adapted and appropriate to the Majority World should allow the church to send a greater number of missionaries throughout the world. With the implementation of better funding models, the total number of missionaries from the Majority World should increase even more, since the traditional model prevents sending them more than it does sending Western missionaries. This means that the "average" missionary in the future will be less and less a white person and more and more a person of color. More importantly, it means that the "average" missionary team will be made up of people from many parts of the world. The global missionary force will better reflect the global church.

Consequently, two other benefits will be possible. Since much of the worldwide church comes from economically disadvantaged countries, missionaries from these countries will be accustomed to living on a much lower salary than their Western colleagues. The funds that are used to send a single Western missionary can be used to send many more missionaries from the Majority World; some, like McQuilkin (1999), would say as many as fifty more. So even if missionary funding in dollar terms does not increase, the number of missionaries will certainly increase because of the economic context of these new missionaries.

Another benefit will be in the ministry to the disadvantaged and poor on the mission field. Western missionaries have great difficulty in reaching these people, since they are unable to live in this context of poverty. On the other hand, missionaries from the Majority World have less difficulty in reaching these people, having themselves already lived very close to this more difficult economic situation. The adaptation will not necessarily be easy, because there will always be an adaptation to the culture and language, but it will be easier for them than for many others who come from a more affluent background.

Linked to this growing number of missionaries, yet another benefit is that there will be a greater number of "restricted" countries that will accept Christian "workers." The more these countries unknowingly accept Christians who will come to work in areas such as economics, education, public health, telecommunications, information technology, and other fields, the more likely these workers will have a positive impact for Jesus Christ. Such strategies have been around for some time, but the funding model for these people will be one less thing that will link them structurally to the

Christian church, making it easier for them to enter into these officially anti-Christian countries incognito. By eliminating the "Christian paper trail," the worker will be more comfortable doing his or her job. The result is unlikely to be an explosion in the growth of the church in these countries, but rather a slow but sure increase in the number of followers who reside there. The church will welcome such an outcome.

With more appropriate funding models, another benefit will be that missionaries will be able to spend all their time ministering instead of worrying about a lack of support or, even worse, leaving the mission field to seek more funds, as was the case with "L" in chapter 3. A missionary who can give 100 percent to her ministry will go through much less worry than a missionary who is often distracted by a lack of funds. These other funding models will not guarantee more fruit in ministry, but they will guarantee a better effort by the missionary, all other things being equal.

Finally, if missionary funding models are better adapted to Majority World contexts, the number of "individualistic" missionaries should decline. Of course, a certain number of individualistic missionaries will remain, because this phenomenon is related more to personality and culture than it is to a simple funding model. But by relying less on the traditional model, the tendency toward individualism in seeking financial support will be diminished, and this will have a positive effect on the life and ministry of the missionary. It should be remembered, however, that other models, such as the tentmaking model, may attract those who are individualistic in nature.

The problem of the independent, individualistic, "I don't need help from anyone else" missionary is not going to go away overnight. But with an increase in the number of missionaries coming from a more communal background and a decrease in the traditional model of fundraising, a less individualistic impact should be felt over time on the mission field. If this is the case, it will be yet another positive benefit in the world of global mission.

Chapter 8

What Does the Bible Say about Missionary Support?

Both the Old and New Testaments give examples of people sent on a mission by God—people such as Abraham, Jonah, Paul, and Barnabas. However, it is the New Testament that speaks much more directly about the principles of mission funding, so the principles we will examine will be taken from its pages. And much space will be given to the modern practices that are drawn from these funding principles.

Who Finances Mission in the New Testament?

There are several examples of missionary financing in the pages of the New Testament. Here are some possibilities that evangelical churches in the Majority World could consider.

Working on the Mission Field

A missionary can meet his own financial needs by working on the field. This can be seen in the life of the Apostle Paul and also in the lives of Aquila and his wife Priscilla, during their stay in Corinth (Acts 18:3). They worked in the trade of tentmaking, which included leather work. Paul also worked with his hands during his time in Ephesus (Acts 20:33–35; 1 Cor 4:12) and Thessalonica (1 Thess 2:9). At the same time, he mentions that Barnabas also worked during his missionary journeys (1 Cor 9:6), without mentioning the nature of his work.

The *Semeur 2000 Study Bible* notes that "contrary to the pagan mentality, Judaism valued manual labour. Professionals were grouped into brotherhoods in which everyone could find a network of relationships and support" (Kuen, Paya, and Buchhold 2005, 1671). Allison Trites (2015, 2013) adds that "according to Jewish custom, a son was given a manual trade, including young men destined for the rabbinate or other professions." It is interesting to note that Acts 18:3 may well indicate that Priscilla was engaged in the same occupation as her husband.[1]

The Fruit of Ministry

A missionary may receive support from those who have responded positively to his message or from the churches he has established, and this support may include food, lodging, etc., as well as finances. New believers provided lodging and food for Peter in Joppa (Acts 9:43; 10:6, 32) and Caesarea (Acts 10:48). Paul planted the church in Corinth. Then he explained thoroughly to the Corinthians that missionaries have the right to receive food and material goods from those to whom they preach the gospel, even though he himself decided not to exercise this right (1 Cor 9:3–18; 2 Cor 12:13).

Paul says that seeking such support was not just some idea he came up with, but that it is actually a command from the Lord (1 Cor 9:14), which is probably a reference to Jesus's words in Luke 10:7. Elsewhere Paul speaks to

---

[1] The *Semeur 2000 Study Bible* (Kuen, Paya, and Buchhold 2005, 1670–71) translates Acts 18:3 by saying, "Since he [Paul] had the same trade as them—they made tents—he stayed with them and they worked together." The *Parole Vivante*, by Alfred Kuen (1976, 408), translates the verse: "Since they were in the same trade as he was, that is, they made tent cloth, they took him as a partner and lodged him with them." It appears that Priscilla worked alongside her husband in the tentmaking business.

the Corinthians about his possible need for accommodation, transportation, etc., and he expects such things from the people he has helped to grow in the faith (1 Cor 16:6, 11; 2 Cor 1:16). Paul applies this same principle to those who serve as pastors or teachers in the local church (Gal 6:6; 1 Tim 5:17–18).[2]

Support from Strangers or Newcomers

A missionary may also be supported by new acquaintances or by churches he has not established himself. Peter was visiting believers in Lydda (Acts 9:32), apparently for the first time, and it is likely that they were attending to his material needs. Paul speaks to the church's faithful members in Rome about his needs related to his upcoming trip to Spain, although he had never visited them before (Rom 15:24). Regarding this missionary journey, Paul tells these believers that he hopes to be "assisted" by them. Similarly, the Apostle John recommends that a local church support some visiting foreign evangelists and missionaries (3 John 5–8). These ideas will be explored later in this chapter.

One-Time Support

Friends, acquaintances, or churches may contribute on a one-time basis to meet an immediate need. In the early days of Paul's ministry, the church at Antioch helped Paul, Barnabas, and other believers with their trip to Jerusalem to attend an important church council (Acts 15:1–3). This most likely covered funds they would need for food and lodging during their trip. Toward the end of his ministry, Paul asked Titus, most likely with help from the church at Crete, to provide for the travel of two co-workers and to "see that they have everything they need" (Titus 3:13).

"Regular" Financial Support

The preceding principles deal generally with one-time needs. But churches can also provide financial support on a regular basis. The church at Philippi sent support to Paul "more than once" during his missionary stay in Thessalonica (Phil 4:16) and once again when he was a prisoner in Rome (Phil 4:18). Paul was grateful for this renewed expression of their feelings toward him, which was seen in the "gifts" that the Philippians had sent through their representative, Epaphroditus. It even seems that the church at Philippi had sent Epaphroditus not only to deliver their gifts but also to assist the apostle as a "co-worker and fellow soldier" (Phil 2:25).

---

[2] First Timothy 5:18 is probably Paul's second reference to Luke 10:7. The first is in 1 Corinthians 9:14, where Paul is speaking about the right of apostles to "receive their living from the gospel." If Paul quotes Jesus in this way, it suggests that the gospels were written and circulated earlier than is usually thought.

While in Corinth, Paul regularly received financial assistance from the churches in Macedonia (2 Cor 11:8–9, *Semeur* [Kuen, Paya, and Buchhold 2005, 1778]).[3] Kuen (1976, 575) supports this idea, translating 2 Corinthians 11:8 as follows: "I have impoverished other churches by accepting subsidies from them to minister among you." Regarding the word *subsidies*, Kuen (1976, 575) notes:

> The Apostle uses a word for the soldier's ration or pay. These are therefore regular and continuous subsidies, presumably from the church at Philippi (cf. Philippians 4:15).

Sending Personnel

Churches can support a ministry by sending personnel, not just money. John Mark was helping Paul and Barnabas, and it seems likely that his church was aware of that help (Acts 12:25; 13:5). The church at Lystra entrusted Timothy to the missionaries Paul and Silas (Acts 16:1–3). Paul traveled with other young men on his journeys (Acts 20:4), presumably with the agreement of their churches. As already mentioned, the church at Philippi entrusted Epaphroditus to Paul while the apostle was in Rome awaiting his audience before the emperor (Phil 2:25, 30). According to Kuen (1976), it is possible that the "assistance" Paul requested for his trip to Spain included personnel (Rom 15:23–24).[4]

Support Sought by a Third Party

Financial or material support may be requested by a third party. Paul asked the church at Corinth to help Timothy with both his stay in Corinth and his subsequent journey back to Paul (1 Cor 16:11). Paul also asked Titus and most likely the churches in Crete to provide fully for Zenas and Apollos, including their journey, and to "see that they lack nothing" (Titus 3:13 ESV). Finally, Paul asked the church in Colossae to welcome Mark if he were to visit (Col 4:10).

Paul felt responsible for his fellow workers, seeking to facilitate their travel and to meet their physical and material needs as much as possible. As an apostle, he believed he had the authority to ask for such things on behalf of his fellow workers.

---

[3] Second Corinthians 11:8 says, "I have robbed other churches that have *regularly* sent me money to minister among you" (emphasis added).

[4] Kuen says that the Greek verb *propempō, to send on one's way/assist on one's journey* meant "to provide directions, recommendations, road provisions, and possibly persons who could accompany" (*Parole Vivante* N.T., 493, footnote).

Humanitarian Emergencies

A local church can also contribute financially to help meet humanitarian emergencies. The church in Antioch sent aid to the brothers and sisters in Judea who were going through a famine (Acts 11:28–30). This church, composed of a large number of non-Jews, was sensitive to the material needs of the all-Jewish church in Jerusalem. Perhaps the fact that Barnabas and Saul were chosen to carry this monetary offering to Jerusalem and were faithful in this task was a factor in their selection by the Holy Spirit for their missionary journey. And the fact that this church in Antioch had already been faithful and generous with its finances may have been an influential factor used by the Holy Spirit to actively launch worldwide mission.

Churches in Corinth, Galatia, and Macedonia also contributed funds to assist the material needs of the saints in Jerusalem (1 Cor 16:1–4; 2 Cor 8 and 9). Coping with a famine or any shortage experienced by brothers and sisters in the faith is a valuable use of church resources. Several additional financial principles are found in these texts, which we will see in the very next section.

What Is the Appropriate Manner of Giving?

In the New Testament there are also several principles about how to contribute financially to God's work; they are not limited to gifts made toward world mission. These principles apply universally to all contributions to the Christian church and its various ministries.

Proportional to Income

The amount of what is given to God is in proportion to one's income (1 Cor 16:2). This means that each person should know their income and then think ahead about how much they can set aside for God's work. When Paul arrived, it would no longer be a matter of collecting money for the financial need in the Jerusalem church, but simply collecting what had already been contributed. Implicit in this passage is the idea of a family budget: knowing ahead of time how much money would generally come in and go out. At the same time, the idea of voluntary donations is also implicit in this text, for each person should "set aside a sum of money." John MacArthur comments (2006, 1769):

> The N.T. never specifies the amount or percentage of what should be given for the Lord's work. Every offering to the Lord must be voluntary and made on the basis of a personal decision.

The goodwill of those who contributed financially is also mentioned in 2 Corinthians 8:10–12 and 9:2. This verse, 1 Corinthians 16:2, also talks about putting money aside on the first day of the week, thus dealing with contributing regularly in order to support ministry, but I have already discussed the principle of regular giving above.

With Generosity

A parallel principle is that of generosity toward God's work. Regarding gifts to the suffering believers in Jerusalem, the Apostle Paul encouraged the Christians in Corinth to "sow generously"—not with reluctance or compulsion, but rather with cheerfulness (2 Cor 9:6–7). If one can give according to one's revenue, according to the preceding principle, there is also a case for giving beyond one's means, as the Christians of Macedonia did (2 Cor 8:3). It is obvious that such generosity can apply to any type of charity, from world mission to donations on behalf of the needy.

We note in several of these examples that those who give are not rich; poor believers can also be generous. This same principle is seen in Acts 11:29, where, in Antioch, "the disciples, as each one was able, decided to provide help for the brothers and sisters living in Judea." We see it again in 2 Corinthians 8:2, where the believers in Macedonia, despite "their extreme poverty," showed a "rich generosity" because of "their overflowing joy." Generosity is more a state of the heart than of the wallet, and this generosity can be applied to any work of God, including world mission.

Multiple People to Manage Money

A final principle is that many people are better than one person when dealing with money. In 1 Corinthians 16:3–4 we see that Paul proposes "the men you approve" to carry the collection to Jerusalem and he volunteers to accompany them. In 2 Corinthians 8 we see that Titus was involved in fundraising (vv. 6, 16, 17), and he was to be accompanied by a brother chosen by the churches (vv. 18–19) and by a third brother who trusted the Corinthians and was zealous for the project (v. 22). The principle of accountability to others for how money is spent is implicit in these two passages.

Reviewing a Key Term

We will continue this chapter on biblical patterns of missionary support by making a few remarks about the Greek word that is often used in the preceding passages—the word προπέμπω (propempō). It is often translated into English as "to send on one's way," but its meaning is broader than merely wishing them safe travels. We will look briefly at five New Testament passages in which this word is used, as it is a key term for understanding missionary funding.

Acts 15:3

As we have seen, Acts 15 recounts the momentous occasion when the church in Antioch decided to send Paul, Barnabas, and a few others to Jerusalem to deal with a serious theological issue. In verse 3, Luke, the author of Acts, says that "The church sent them on their way..." This passage shows that when a local church is confronted by a serious theological problem, it has the right—even the duty—to do everything possible to help solve it. In Acts chapter 15, the church of Antioch sent its greatest leaders to Jerusalem to participate in the council that was being convened. Given who it was that traveled to Jerusalem, it seems likely that the church in Antioch did more than escort them out to the city gates. Presumably the church of Antioch provided food for the beginning of the journey, and a certain amount of money for the journey on foot to Jerusalem, covering the costs of lodging, food, etc., which are more than just transportation costs.

It should be noted in passing that those who received this assistance were members of the same church that offered the support; that is, the donors provided for the material needs of some of their own members. This fact could have motivated them to be especially generous.

Romans 15:24

We also mentioned this passage in Romans 15 earlier. In verse 24, the Apostle Paul writes, "I hope to see you while passing through and to have you assist me on my journey [to Spain]." Here Paul expresses his desire to visit the church in Rome, a church he had never visited before. He would like to pass through Rome to see the believers there and then go on to Spain, where he would, it is assumed, "preach the gospel where Christ was not known" (Rom 15:20). It would not be a short visit from Rome to Spain.

Given the supposed purpose and scope of this trip to Spain, the church in Rome will enjoy the Apostle Paul's company, and then they are supposed to "assist [him] on [his] journey." Once again, different versions of the Bible translate *propempō* using various terms, but they especially use something along the line of "help me on my journey."

But what kind of help are we talking about here? We have seen Kuen's remark earlier, where he says that this help is not limited to financial assistance but also includes practical advice, material provisions, and even people who could accompany Paul. Perhaps his boldness in asking so much of these brothers and sisters comes from the fact that Paul knew some of the people in this church quite well, which is evident when one reads his greetings in chapter 16 of the epistle. But it goes without saying that a missionary journey into a new part of the world will necessitate a more complete type of resourcing than just a few coins.

1 Corinthians 16:6, 11

The word *propempō* is found twice in 1 Corinthians 16, first in verse 6 and then in verse 11. It is translated in various ways, but most commonly by "help [me]" and "send [me/him] on [my/his] way." In this passage the Apostle Paul wants help first for himself and then for his co-worker, Timothy. Note that Paul does not *ask* them for help; he essentially *tells* them to help. It is almost as if he is giving them an order, especially concerning Timothy, since he uses the imperative form of the verb.

We notice in this passage that the desired "help" goes beyond mere financial assistance, since Paul seems to expect the provision of lodging for a period of several months. It would be logical to think that the Corinthians would also provide him with a bed and food during his stay with them. In addition, he is counting on them to provide financially for his subsequent trip in the spring, a trip whose purpose was not to evangelize Gentiles, but rather to provide financial assistance to the believers in Jerusalem who were going through material hardship. It was therefore more of a social or humanitarian journey that Paul had in mind.

We therefore conclude that this help coming from the Corinthians concerns more than pocket money, and that it is intended for more than one person. We could deduce that the apostle will spend his "home assignment" in Corinth and that the local church will provide everything he needs, as well as the necessary means for him to resume his journey afterward. In addition, the church will help a personal friend and co-worker of Paul's so that he, too, can continue his journey and return to Paul and their missionary team.

Titus 3:13–14

Although the verb *propempō* is found only in Titus 3:13, verse 14 completes the idea of supporting two missionary co-workers of the Apostle Paul. In verse 13, Paul tells Titus to take care of the journey that his two co-workers, Zenas and Apollos, will take. Various versions of the Bible translate the Greek word *propempō* with "speed them on their way" (ESV); "help them with their trip" (NLT); "help them on their way" (NIV); "give them a hearty send-off" (MSG). Once again, Paul does not *ask* Titus to do this; he expects him to do it.

It is interesting to note that Paul gives this imperative to Titus himself, as if this church leader should cover the travel expenses of these other two men all by himself. Perhaps this may explain the next verse, where Paul hastens to add that all the other believers should participate in "doing what is good" to provide for the pressing needs of these mission colleagues.

We can therefore draw the conclusion that church leaders must act on two fronts with regard to mission. They can participate personally, and they can motivate others to participate as well. But in both cases, Paul expects donors to be generous, because they are expected to contribute so that Zenas and Apollos "have everything they need." Even if these believers in Crete are new converts, which is probably the case, Paul wants them to learn to be generous.

Apollos was actively involved in a church-planting ministry, both in Ephesus and Corinth (Acts 18:24–28; 1 Cor 3). He was an ethnic Egyptian, a man skilled in public debate who had "a thorough knowledge of the Scriptures." As for "Zenas the lawyer," however, Titus 3:13 is the only verse in the Bible that speaks of him. It is not known why Zenas was traveling with Apollos, but it is quite possible that he was performing some kind of administrative function, given his legal title. Some commentators see him as an expert in Roman law; others see him as an expert in Jewish law and hence a co-worker with Paul in evangelism. It is impossible to come to a definitive conclusion on this question. But if the first conclusion is correct, it would mean that Paul encouraged financial "help" not only for a missionary co-worker (Apollos), but also for someone who may have been an administrative or legal assistant (Zenas).

In verse 14, Paul says that these new believers must "devote themselves to doing what is good, in order to provide for urgent needs and not live unproductive lives." The apostle frames this contribution to mission by the principle of participating in good works, which is one of the main themes of this letter to Titus. Therefore, generosity can benefit not only those who go to the mission field, but it can also help the giver to lead a productive life.

3 John 5–8

The last passage I will examine is found in one of the shortest epistles of the New Testament—3 John. The verb *propempō* is found in verse 6, and some different versions translate the context in the following way: "send them on their journey" (ESV); "help them on their way" (Message); "send them on their way" (NIV and NASB); "continue providing for them" (NLT). In this little letter, the Apostle John thanks his friend, Gaius, for having welcomed "traveling missionaries" (v. 7 AMP), or "traveling teachers" (v. 5 NLT). John congratulates Gaius for his hospitality toward people who are brothers and sisters in the Lord but who are also "strangers to you" (v. 5).

This hospitality is not all that Gaius must provide, however. John also encourages Gaius to provide for their travel once they are ready to leave his home and continue their mission elsewhere. These are the two responsibilities of Christians toward those who serve the Lord by faith: "It is therefore our (Christian) duty to welcome such men and to support them. In this way we will collaborate in what they do to spread the truth" (3 John 8, Kuen 1976, 784).

This passage clearly shows that it takes a whole team of people to participate in mission: those who go out as missionaries and those who contribute by other means, such as prayer, hospitality, and finances. One cannot be effective without the other.

To summarize the ideas that come from the Greek word *propempō* and "helping missionaries on their way," I offer the following table.

How to "Send" Someone in Mission
(Greek word: προπέμπω, *propempō*)

Reference	Who "sends"?	Who is "sent"?	The "sending" includes...	For what purpose?
Acts 15:3	Paul's "home church" in Antioch	Paul, Barnabas, other believers	Food, supplies, finances	Solving a theological/ecclesiastical problem
Romans 15:24	The church at Rome, which Paul had not founded or visited	Paul	Finances, information, advice, perhaps personnel	Missionary trip to Spain (see Rom 15:23–24)
1 Corinthians 16:6, 11 (also 2 Corinthians 1:16)	A church founded by Paul	Paul, Timothy	Lodging, food for Paul, means of travel for Timothy	Missionary "home assignment" for Paul, Timothy's trip, Paul's upcoming trip to Jerusalem to help needy believers
Titus 3:13–14	A church that Paul may have founded; Titus as church leader	Zenas the lawyer, Apollos	Finances, "daily necessities" ("Do everything you can to ... see that they have everything they need.")	Administrative/legal assistance and/or an evangelistic mission

Reference	Who "sends"?	Who is "sent"?	The "sending" includes...	For what purpose?
3 John 5–8	The church of a spiritual friend/son	Unknown evangelists and mission-aries	Housing, food, supplies, finances ("Send them on their way in a manner worthy of God.")	Evangelistic mission

What Is the Biblical Evidence for the Role of a Majority-World Church in Mission?

Although the African presence in the New Testament does not address the financial aspect of mission, I believe it is important for the church in the Majority World today to see the African presence in the New Testament and how it has influenced global mission. It is obvious that most of these other regions—Central and East Asia, Latin America, and Eastern Europe—were not known or were hardly known by the New Testament writers. Although these other regions of the world were not explicitly mentioned, I would maintain that Africa represents the rest of the Majority World when it comes to its biblical presence.

Even the African presence in the New Testament is not easy to identify. The Ethiopian "eunuch" in Acts 8 is a well-known African follower of Jesus Christ, but he quickly disappeared from the scene. Apart from this man, what other Africans appear during the time of the early church? Three passages in the book of Acts reveal other people, allowing us to better answer this question.

Acts 2

When the Holy Spirit came upon the disciples, "tongues" are mentioned several times. Two Greek words are used for "tongues" in Acts 2. The first is the word *glossa* (verses 3, 4, and 11), which is also used in 1 Corinthians 14, where Paul teaches about the gift of speaking in tongues. The context in 1 Corinthians helps us understand that *glossa* refers to ecstatic and unknown languages. However, in Acts 2 the context is very clear that the "tongues" spoken of refer to known languages. The crowd was amazed because, according to verse 11, the disciples were "declaring the wonders of God in our own tongues (*glossa*)."

The second word for "tongues" is *dialektos* (verses 6 and 8), from which the English word *dialect* is derived. Once again, it is clear that the disciples were speaking in known languages, as verse 6 speaks of "their own language" and verse 8 speaks of "our native language" (each time *dialektos*).[5]

Those who listened to the disciples came from all over the known world—fifteen different regions are mentioned, two of which are in Africa: Egypt and the neighboring territory around the city of Cyrene, in eastern Libya. People from Asia and Europe are also on the list.

These pilgrims who came to Jerusalem for Pentecost were "God-fearing Jews" (verse 5). An important question must be asked here: Were they Israelites who had immigrated to these different regions and were now back home? Or were they natives of these fifteen different regions? There are two reasons why the answer to both parts of this question is yes.

One reason is that verse 11 calls them "Jews and converts to Judaism." A "Jew" was obviously a person who came from Israel. But the technical word used here for "converts to Judaism" is "proselytes." A proselyte is defined as a convert to Judaism who comes from a Gentile—i.e., non-Jewish—background. This word comes from the Hebrew term *gēr*, which primarily refers to a foreign resident (Trebilco 2010). Thus, a proselyte was initially a Gentile, someone who came from a country other than Israel. So we see that those present at this festival were both Israelites and foreigners.

A second reason that supports a large foreign presence is that the disciples declared the wonders of God in their "native language." What was the native language of an Israelite who had immigrated elsewhere? It was Hebrew/Aramaic. If those mentioned were Israelites who had only immigrated to these other parts of the empire, their mother tongue would have been the same mother tongue as that of the disciples. There would have been no need for a miracle of the Holy Spirit to speak to them in other languages. The fact that the disciples needed to speak in other native languages shows us that many of these people were native-speakers of those languages, hence natives of those regions.

As for Africa, this means that there were not only Israelites who had immigrated to Egypt, but also Egyptians who spoke the Egyptian language. There were not only Israelites who lived in Libya, but also Libyans who might

---

[5] Some commentators believe the miracle was in the "hearing" rather than in the "speaking"—that is, the disciples were speaking in ecstatic *glossa*, but the hearers miraculously heard them speaking in their native languages. But the question must be asked, if the hearers actually heard another language, how could they claim, much less prove, that such a language was *not* being spoken? All they would know is what they heard. There is no indication in this passage that other people heard it differently. To me, such an interpretation seems to be based more on what some people want to believe instead of on what the text actually says in this chapter.

have spoken a Berber language. Craig Keener (1993, 322–23) says in *The IVP Bible Background Commentary*:

> Although these are Jews, they are culturally and linguistically members of many nations; thus, even from the church's inception as an identifiable community, the Spirit proleptically moved the church into multicultural diversity under Christ's lordship.

The miracle of Pentecost is that the disciples were able to speak in everyone else's "own language" (verse 6) and in the "native language" (verse 8) of these different indigenous peoples. That fact supports the multi-ethnic composition of the listeners at Pentecost. Otherwise, no language-related miracle would have been necessary.

This passage therefore confirms that on the day the church was born, Asians, Africans, and Europeans were present, participating in the birth. Their presence was somewhat hidden, but it was nonetheless real. These visitors from Africa, Asia, and Europe may have been a minority, but they were a significant minority nonetheless. The miracle of the Holy Spirit, where the disciples spoke in other known languages, reveals the presence of these other ethnic groups.

Acts 11

In verses 19 to 21 we see the beginning of cross-cultural mission. Because of the persecution that followed Stephen's death (see Acts 8), believers scattered throughout the region, preaching the gospel in Phoenicia (modern Lebanon), Cyprus (an island in the Mediterranean Sea), and Antioch (in Syria). Yet these believers only preached the good news to Jews. But some men from Cyprus and Cyrene (a large city in northeastern Libya; see Acts 2:10) decided to go to Antioch, the third-largest city in the Roman Empire, after Rome and Alexandria, and began sharing the good news of Jesus directly with Greeks—i.e., Gentiles—also. It should be noted that there were no "apostles" with them; it seems that they made this decision of their own free will.

In these three verses, we see three major turning points in the history of the church:

1) For the first time in the book of Acts, the gospel is preached in the zone called "the ends of the earth" (see Acts 1:8). The mission field has changed.

2) For the first time in the book of Acts, those who preach the gospel are not believers from Israel. The messenger has changed.

3) For the first time in the book of Acts, the gospel is proclaimed directly to Gentiles, showing that it is not necessary to become a Jew before giving oneself to Jesus. The audience has changed.

In my opinion, these three verses, because of the decisive turning points they represent, are the most important verses in the book of Acts. And who was responsible for these great turning points? "Men from Cyprus and Cyrene" (Acts 11:20)—Cyrene being a large city in Africa. It should not be forgotten, however, that Cyrene was a Greek colony in Africa and that many Jews also resided there. It is therefore likely that, among the first people to take Christ's Great Commission seriously and dare to do something radical, there were both Libyan and Cypriot believers, and perhaps even some Greek believers as well. While all initially immigrated to Jerusalem as converts to Judaism, at some point in time after Pentecost they became followers of Jesus.

These people chose Antioch of their own free will, breaking with the precedent of waiting for an apostolic initiative. But they did so because "the Lord's hand was with them" (verse 21); this was sufficient divine authorization. They obeyed the Lord's guidance in their lives, and in fact this is the key to effective missionary service. When it comes to cross-cultural mission, these Majority World believers were among the very first to participate.

Acts 13
According to Acts 13:1, there were five leaders in the church at Antioch: Barnabas, Simeon, Lucius, Manaen, and Saul. They were the teachers and prophets/preachers in the church. Two of the five were from Africa: "Simeon called Niger" and "Lucius of Cyrene." *Niger* is the Latin word for "black." Most commentators maintain that, because of his nickname, Simeon was a black African and not an ethnic Jew who lived in North Africa.[6] Another important question is to ask why Simeon had a Latin nickname. The parts of North Africa that were oriented toward the Greek world were Egypt and Eastern Libya. But the part of North Africa that was oriented to the Latin world was Western Libya, Tunisia, and Algeria. While "Simeon" is obviously a Jewish name, perhaps having a Latin nickname means that Simeon was a black man who came from the region that would be part of Tunisia or even Algeria today.

As for Lucius, he also came from Africa, but it is impossible to know if he was an ethnic African, a Greek immigrant who lived there (since Cyrene was a large Greek colony), or an ethnic Jew (since there was a large Jewish quarter in Cyrene). As in the case of "Simon from Cyrene" who carried Jesus's cross (Luke 23:26), it is impossible to prove whether Lucius was an African, an ethnic Jew, or a Greek. All are possible. But we do know that Lucius had spent part—and perhaps a significant part—of his life in Africa, since he is identified as Lucius "of Cyrene."

---

[6] It should not be forgotten that some Africans in this region, such as the Berbers, were not black. The word *African* is not necessarily synonymous with "black."

The fact that the church at Antioch became the missionary church *par excellence* of the New Testament should not surprise us. This church had its own roots in cross-cultural mission, as discussed above. And its own leaders were a multicultural mix of people from Asia and Africa. It seems logical, then, that these "prophets and teachers" at Antioch contributed to Barnabas and Saul's missionary preparation, although that is impossible to prove. But if they were sensitive to the guidance of the Holy Spirit—which they were—it could be that these other leaders had a real heart for mission and that they taught accordingly in the Antioch church.

We later see in Acts 15:35, after Paul and Barnabas returned from their first missionary trip, that these two apostles "and many others" were teaching and preaching the good news of "the word of the Lord." The question arises: Who trained these "many others" to teach and proclaim the good news of Jesus during the two-year absence of Paul and Barnabas while they were on their missionary journey? A good hypothesis is that the three leaders who remained in Antioch—Lucius, Simeon, and Manaen—did this training. Acts 15:35 seems to confirm their ability to train others in teaching and preaching in the local church and community.

It is often thought that mission began in Acts 13, when Barnabas and Saul went to Cyprus. But a closer look at the text shows that cross-cultural mission had already begun before Barnabas and Saul ever left Antioch. Moreover, it's possible that men from Africa had a missionary impact on the lives of these two great apostles, since the church at Antioch had been founded by missionaries from another part of the world. Barnabas and Saul were sent to help establish a church that had been birthed through mission.

Finally, we see that in Acts 2, on the day the church was born, that Africans and Asians were there. In Acts 11, when some of the first believers were pressured by persecution to leave Jerusalem and evangelize another part of the world, Christians from Libya and Cyprus were present. In Acts 13, when church leaders prepared to send others on mission, Africans helped.

The known world in New Testament times consisted of the continents of Africa, Asia, and Europe. In Acts 8, the Ethiopian eunuch, a government official from Africa, decided to follow Jesus. In Acts 9, Saul of Tarsus, a Jewish Pharisee from Asia (Asia Minor), decided to follow Jesus. In Acts 10, Cornelius of the Italian Regiment, a Roman centurion from Europe, decided to follow Jesus. Through these passages, the Holy Spirit is telling us that Christianity is a religion for the whole world, for all the people groups on this planet. While Africa is specifically highlighted in these three passages, the inclusion of Cyprus shows that Asia is also a player in world mission.

By extension, these passages show that the Majority World has its part to play in what God is doing around the world today.

Today the church in the Majority World has reached maturity. There are churches in Central and East Asia, Eastern Europe, and Latin America that are mature enough, rooted enough in the Word of God, sensitive enough to the guidance of the Holy Spirit, and resourceful enough to make a worldwide impact for Jesus Christ. Today's Majority World church does not have to seek a new path to do so. It can move forward by reclaiming the path of its biblical past: evangelism, cross-cultural mission, and preparing others for mission. And all that took place before those who are usually called the "first missionaries" in the book of Acts ever left their "home church" in Antioch.

Chapter 9

A New Economic Standing

Since the year 2000, a significant number of countries in the Majority World have gained a new economic standing. While some countries (such as Venezuela, Democratic Republic of the Congo, and Myanmar, to name a few) continue to face financial decline due to political insecurity or misguided economic policies, others have made important strides.

Economic Growth

Economic growth is often measured by gross domestic product (GDP), and it is usually measured in terms of "real growth"—that is, nominal GDP that is inflation-adjusted to show "the value of all goods and services produced by an economy in a given year" (Ganti 2023). Such "real" GDP growth is also referred to as "GDP-PPP—GDP with purchasing power parity." GDP is often shown in per capita figures instead of overall amounts per country, making the numbers a little easier to understand.

It can be tricky to look at such results when it comes to real growth from one year to the next, since real GDP growth is usually shown as a percentage. For instance, in his article on Africa's economic outlook, Tom Collins (2022) states that "The [International Monetary] Fund says that the top five economies to grow in Africa will be Seychelles, Rwanda, Mauritius, Niger and Benin which all look set to hit above 6% growth." He goes on to note that "Nigeria, Angola and South Africa are all in the bottom 10 countries for GDP growth at 2.7%, 2.4% and 2.2% respectively." The impression these statistics give is that it would be more economically beneficial to live in Niger than in South Africa in 2022.

This is where one has to be careful in interpreting results. On one hand, Niger's 6 percent growth looks really good, while South Africa's 2.2 percent growth looks rather dismal. But Niger is ranked 187 out of 192 countries in terms of GDP per capita with purchasing power parity (Ventura 2022). We need to remember that when you have virtually nothing to start with, it's far easier to increase by a larger percentage. A 6 percent growth rate for Niger only comes to an additional $79 per capita PP. But South Africa is ranked 99 on the same scale, and its very meager 2.2 percent economic growth equals an increase of $338, or more than four times Niger's "top economy" money per capita. So we see that while the percentage figures look good, the dollar figures give a different—and perhaps a more realistic—picture of the situation.

When looking at percentages, a better solution is to look at regional economic growth instead of individual countries' growth, as there is rarely one extremely wealthy country in the midst of poor ones, or one extremely poor country in the midst of wealthy ones.

The projected economic forecasts for various parts of the Majority World are given below for 2022:

- Asian emerging market and developing countries[1] (IMF 2022)   5.4%
- Latin America and the Caribbean[2] (Romero 2022)   3.0%
- Middle East and North Africa[3] (World Bank 2022a)   5.2%

---

[1] These fifteen countries consist of Bangladesh, Brunei, Cambodia, China, India, Indonesia, Laos, Malaysia, Myanmar, Mongolia, Nepal, Philippines, Sri Lanka, Thailand, and Vietnam.

[2] Included here are the thirty-three countries in all of South America, Central America (including Mexico), and the Caribbean.

[3] These nineteen countries consist of Algeria, Bahrain, Djibouti, Egypt, Iran, Iraq, Jordan, Kuwait, Lebanon, Libya, Morocco, Oman, Palestinian Territories, Qatar, Saudi Arabia, Syria, Tunisia, UAE, and Yemen.

- Eastern Europe and Central Asia[4] (World Bank 2022b)   −3.0%
- East and Southern Sub-Saharan Africa[5] (World Bank 2022c)   3.1%
- West and Central Sub-Saharan Africa (World Bank 2022c)   4.2%

It is helpful to compare these projected growth rates to the world's stronger economies, so here are some other projections for 2022:

- Advanced Asian economies[6] (IMF 2022)   2.7%
- Asia as a whole (IMF 2022)   4.9%
- European Union (Clark 2022)   2.7%
- USA, first two quarters of 2022 (BEA 2022a)   −1.6% and −0.9%
- USA, second half of 2022 (Reuters 2022)   2.4%

Without going into various details that could be discussed here (such as the war between Russia and Ukraine, which is skewing the Eastern Europe and Central Asia results), suffice it to say that the projected growth rates for much of the Majority World surpass that of the economies considered to be more stable. While that fact points to a positive outlook for the economies of the Majority World, it is a fact that needs to be taken for what it's worth, since, as stated above, a strong economy's lower growth represents a more significant increase than a weaker economy's higher growth in terms of per capita purchasing power parity (PPP).

Investments

Investments in the economies of the Majority World have changed significantly due to the COVID-19 pandemic. Prior to 2020, Asia and the Pacific had alone received the colossal amount of $1.5 trillion in foreign direct investment, abbreviated as FDI (UN-ESCAP 2021). Latin America and Africa received far less than that, but Latin America regularly received more than $100 billion annually in FDI between 2012 and 2019 (UN-ECLAC 2022), and Africa received between $48 and $70 billion annually between 2010 and 2019—and that was solely from the United States (Statista 2022a).

---

[4] Here the World Bank does not distinguish between Eastern Europe and Central Asia in their overall projections. The twenty-three countries included here are Albania, Armenia, Azerbaijan, Belarus, Bosnia and Herzegovina, Bulgaria, Croatia, Georgia, Hungary, Kazakhstan, Kosovo, Kyrgyzstan, Moldova, Montenegro, North Macedonia, Poland, Romania, Russia, Serbia, Tajikistan, Turkey, Ukraine, and Uzbekistan. Turkmenistan has been excluded due to lack of reliable data.

[5] This particular World Bank site did not list which countries are included in East and Southern sub-Saharan Africa, saying simply that these countries stretch "from the Red Sea in the North to the Cape of Good Hope in the South." West and Central Africa would be all the remaining countries in Africa south of the Sahara.

[6] The seven countries included in this category are Australia, Hong Kong, Japan, Korea, New Zealand, Singapore, and Taiwan.

Eastern Europe received between $55 and $61 billion prior to the pandemic (BEA 2022b). When the pandemic came in full force in 2020, all of those numbers dropped, except for Eastern Europe's, which increased to just over $74 billion (BEA 2022b).

As COVID eased, Majority World investments began to rebound in 2021. Eastern Europe continued to improve, with FDI coming in at over $77 billion (BEA 2022b), while Latin America once again surpassed $100 billion (UN-ECLAC 2022) and African FDI reached a record $83 billion (UNCTAD 2022). Asia seems to have once again surpassed the trillion-dollar mark in FDI (UN-ESCAP 2022). While Asia and Latin America have not yet attained their pre-pandemic levels, Africa and Eastern Europe have already surpassed theirs.

Remittances

An additional element worth mentioning here is the money sent to Majority World countries by what is known as the diaspora—that is, workers who have immigrated to countries outside their home continent. It is common knowledge that immigrants are very generous; those who leave their countries to find work in Europe, North America, or Asia send money regularly to their families back home. But the size of these remittances is often surprising. For a large number of countries, the money sent by electronic transfer to home countries exceeds the amount that the home country receives in foreign aid. The World Bank (Ong 2022) states that

> remittance flows to low- and middle-income countries (LMICs) are expected to increase by 4.2 percent this year to reach $630 billion. This follows an almost record recovery of 8.6 percent in 2021.

This same report shows that remittances have made "strong gains" in every part of the Majority World. Such generosity by those in the diaspora is something the Majority World church should take into account. There are undoubtedly many Christians in the diaspora who would be very open to programs and projects that advance the kingdom of God through Majority World missionaries.

Risks

Despite all these examples of economic growth and the many cases of investment in the Majority World, does this mean that these countries no longer have any financial problems? Of course not. Many problems still exist. Jake Bright and Aubrey Hruby (2015, 112) explain:

> We see three causes of disruption that could hinder the revolutionary economic advances of some African countries: massive unemployment

and public discord; institutional inability to align the motivations of the hyper-rich with the common good; rare and unexpected changes in the market.

These authors understand that a number of good statistics doesn't mean that everything is rosy. There are still obstacles to overcome. Other observers agree. Ben Barber (2018) notes that the governance problem in Southeast Asia is getting worse:

> Authoritarian rule is spreading among Southeast Asian nations today. In Thailand, Myanmar (Burma), Malaysia, the Philippines, Singapore and Indonesia, a new breed of autocrat is taking root. … Tough, flexible and expansive authoritarian regimes such as Vietnam have inspired former U.S. allies in Southeast Asia such as Thailand and the Philippines to stifle the press, curb democracy and quell critical voices that embarrass those in power.

In addition to economic and governance issues, security instabilities are far too prevalent. For instance, one website featuring the article titled "Security Challenges in Latin America" (RANE-Worldview 2022) speaks to numerous issues, all of which date from the last twelve months:

- Inflation-induced unrest in Peru;
- Anti-corruption push in Honduras;
- Rebel groups in Colombia;
- Cartels target Mexico's resorts;
- An anti-gang state of emergency in El Salvador.

These remarks show that no part of the Majority World is immune to these negative factors. But in spite of the fact that such negativity is real, the Majority World has made significant economic progress in recent years and is likely to continue to do so. With stronger economies and increasing investment, the number of jobs will increase, development will progress, and economic and financial opportunities for employees will grow.

The business community already seems to recognize the Majority World for its great financial promise. Its vision for the Majority World is almost limitless. Certain aspects of its economy are more developed than in the past, and thus it should not be perceived in the same way as in the past. We will now look at four of these aspects—but without going into great detail, since an entire book could be written on each of the four.

Telecommunications

The sector that is probably the most impressive is the telecommunications sector. With the advent of cellular phones, telephones in the Majority World have jumped over many generations of technology at once. According to

Bright and Hruby (2015), about 70 percent of Africans south of the Sahara own a cell phone. Based on my own experience in urban Abidjan, I estimate that close to 90 percent of the population in the city own a cell phone. And this is only the beginning, as smartphones, which are much more powerful than the first cell phones, are starting to gain more market share. Bright and Hruby (2015, 187–88) say that:

> Africa's conversion to smartphones and other internet devices will present more than one global opportunity for telephone companies. It will completely transform business and social activity on the continent, especially with the improvement of broadband. Smartphones will become the central platform for almost everything in Africa.

One might wonder if this idea, published in 2015, has not already been attained. With a smartphone, customers can buy fuel at a gas station. With a smartphone, they can pay their electricity bill. With a smartphone, they can transfer money to someone else; they can receive video messages from their friends; they can participate in a training course from another continent while driving down a highway in Africa; they can receive a warning about an unsafe incident that is taking place in a certain area of their city; they can order an evening meal and have it delivered to their home; they can reserve and purchase an airline ticket and receive the boarding pass. This list could go on and on.

In Asia, the telecommunications world is even more pervasive and astounding. People from the Philippines spend more time on their smartphones than residents of any other country, averaging 5 hours 47 minutes on their phone every day. The top two countries for smartphone usage are in East Asia (the Philippines and Thailand), and four of the top ten are from this same region (Howarth 2023).

As for the rest of the Majority World, four of the top ten countries for smartphone usage are in Latin America, while two of the top seven countries are in Africa. Of those countries that exceed the global average of 3 hours 43 minutes per day, six are in Asia, five are in Africa, four are in Latin America, and three are in the Middle East. No countries from Europe, North America, or Oceania are in this group. It can also be noted that the top two countries in Europe for smartphone usage are Romania and Russia, both in Eastern Europe. This shows us that the Majority World has embraced the new telecommunications world in ways that surpass the more economically prosperous Western world. With the exception of Taiwan, no country from Western Europe, North America, the Far East, or Oceania is even in the top twenty in terms of smartphone usage.

According to an article on smartphone usage statistics (Marko M. 2022):

> [The] UN's International Telecommunications Union (ITU) came out with a mind-blowing revelation … that there are more telephones on Earth now than there are people. … The research concludes by adding that the proliferation of phones is currently outpacing the growth of the human population, meaning that this trend will continue in the future.

Going forward, it is easy to imagine that smartphones will play a larger and larger role in the life of the common person, both urban and rural, in the Majority World.

Information Technology and E-Commerce

Advances in the field of telecommunications owe their success to another sector of the economy, that of information technology—better known by the abbreviation IT. Without information technology, communication would never have had the opportunity to benefit from these advances.

Many information start-ups exist in East Africa, especially in Kenya—which has acquired the name "Silicon Savannah" (taken from the name "Silicon Valley" in California, where many small information companies are located). These small information companies use technology in smartphones to enable consumers to do most anything they can imagine. For example, a farmer can put small chips in the ears of his cows or goats to track not only the movement of his herds, but also the health of each animal. Or a city dweller can use his smartphone to avoid traffic jams on his way home from work or, with some new apps like Ushahidi, avoid hot spots and violence during elections or other major events.

In terms of technological development, however, Asia is the world's new powerhouse. Oliver Tonby et al. (2020) state that

> over the past decade, [Asia] has developed and deepened its technological capabilities and infrastructure rapidly, accounting for a large share of global growth in technology company revenue start-up funding, spending on R&D, and patents filed.

Without going into extensive detail, let me cite some other key findings from their report:

- The number of internet users in Asia has grown more than the number elsewhere, and the region is now home to half the global total.
- App downloads have grown more in the region than in the rest of the world, reflecting Asia's mobile-first approach to the internet. The region accounted for 41 percent of all mobile-app downloads in 2019.

- Asia accounts for 42 percent of global start-up investment in AI [artificial intelligence] technologies and has a 48-percent share of AI strong patents.
- China and India are home to more than two-thirds of urban technology hotspots … but most other Asian countries have at least one hotspot city, typically the capital.
- Among the world's top five thousand companies, Asian companies contributed 49 percent of the revenue in the information technology sector.
- Asia—especially China and India—will drive growth in consumer markets, and therefore demand for IT services is expected to rise sharply.

In other words, with all the progress Asia has made in the area of information technology in the last ten years, I get the impression that "We ain't seen nothin' yet!"

Perhaps the most dramatic offshoot of information technology can be seen in the area of e-commerce. In Africa, more and more people are buying their household items or clothes on the Jumia platform, which also provides home delivery. In 2016 Jumia, under the supervision of Africa Internet Group (AIG) in Nigeria, announced a partnership with Axa, "enabling the French group to become the exclusive provider of insurance products and services on the Jumia platform as well as on all of AIG's other online and mobile platforms" (Choisnet 2016, 6).

The list of what can be purchased on Jumia could be continued almost ad infinitum. Other e-commerce platforms for Africa include Takealot, Kilimall, Konga, and BidorBuy (SLA 2022).

But Jumia in Africa is nothing in size compared to Alibaba in Asia. Indeed, Alibaba has become the king of e-commerce. Brian O'Connell (2020) states that "For all the accolades for US–based internet-technology giants like Amazon.com and Facebook, the real king of the digital hill lies thousands of miles to the east in China—the home of Alibaba."

O'Connell continues by saying that it was Jack Ma, Alibaba's "visionary founder who saw a marketing opening in internet-based e-commerce and took full advantage." In terms of numbers, a leading provider of market research and consumer data called Statista (2022b) reports that approximately 2.35 billion people used e-commerce in Asia in 2021, with that number expected to hit 3.1 billion in 2025. And e-commerce, while originally dependent upon home computers, is now using smartphones and other mobile devices much more than computers.

The new term "m-commerce," short for "mobile commerce," is being used more and more frequently to refer to the buying and selling of products using a smartphone. S. Ganbold (2021) states that "M-commerce has also experienced a rise in the Asia-Pacific region, with consumers in Indonesia, Thailand, and the Philippines displaying the highest m-commerce penetration throughout the region." This demonstrates that it is not only the most advanced Asian nations that are benefiting from these new developments in e-commerce.

Naturally, Latin America has joined the e-commerce bandwagon. The Argentina-based online marketplace, Mercado Libre, is the most-visited site for e-commerce in all of Latin America. Stephanie Chevalier (2022) reports:

> In addition to being among the most used e-commerce mobile apps in Brazil, the auction site has become the second most popular online retailer in Peru. During the coronavirus outbreak, the company saw its sales in Chile, Colombia, and Mexico double, thereby securing its reign in the regional market, ahead of global giant Amazon.

In fact, Chevalier's figures show that Mercado Libre receives almost four times as many monthly visits as does Amazon. Such examples demonstrate very clearly that the Majority World has made giant leaps forward in terms of commercial buying power.

Banking

Another sector mentioned in an earlier chapter is banking. In the Majority World, this sector works very well in certain advanced Asian countries, but the situation is different in most of the other countries. Khalid Umar (2021), the head of strategic planning at the CAREC Institute, estimates that 1.7 billion people in the world do not have access to banking services. With regard to traditional banking before the advent of new technologies, about 80 percent of Africans did not have access to traditional banking (Fiano 2017), due to a lack of secure wages or land that could be used as collateral.

Hector Galvan (2021) reports that Latin America is facing similar circumstances. He states that in Latin America, "Up to 65% of adults are unbanked, meaning that these individuals do not have access to many financial services and things like a debit card, credit card, or even a bank account."

While over 90 percent of the citizens of Mongolia, as a rare exception, have a bank account, most countries in Central Asia are below 50 percent of their population—with Pakistan, the sixth most populous country in the world, coming in at only 21 percent (Umar 2021). Banking services are lagging behind in much of the Majority World.

But this great need has turned into a great opportunity for many banks. These statistics show that there is a huge customer base that banks can still attract, and increasingly "mobile banking" is providing the convenient services desired by its customers. According to Hichem Ben Yaïche and Guillaume Weill-Raynal (2016, 14), Boubker Jaï, the general manager of Attijariwafa Bank (Morocco), says:

> The challenge for us, everywhere on the [African] continent, is to be in perfect coherence with local needs. It is not only a question of duplicating products that have worked elsewhere, but above all, of understanding the market well and proposing adapted products. In terms of functionality, of course, but also in terms of price.

Umar (2021) concurs, stating:

> Digital banking, which uses mobile and internet technology, offers an opportunity for reaching the financially excluded and underserved segments of the population [in Central Asia], particularly in remote regions and communities. It has the potential to transform the financial inclusion landscape by offering cost-effective and easily accessible financial services.

These quotes show that banks are looking to adapt to the real needs of their customers and to do so at an affordable price.

However, where the banks have been slow to adapt to the current information-technology revolution, telecommunication companies have stepped in. For example, in Kenya, the major telecommunications company, Safaricom, has initiated the M-Pesa service—the letter M stands for "mobile," and *pesa* is the Swahili word for "money."

Within two years, M-Pesa had more than six million customers and was transferring more than $1.5 billion each year (Bright and Hruby 2015). This new method of money transfer greatly increases security for merchants, who no longer have to carry a lot of cash on their person. It also helps parents pay their children's school fees more easily.

The equivalent of one-third of Kenya's GDP goes through M-Pesa, making Kenya one of the most advanced countries in terms of a nonmonetary economy (Bright and Hruby 2015). Yana Emets (2017) reports that since its creation in 2007, M-Pesa has expanded its services as far away as Afghanistan, India, and Albania. And many countries in Africa have their equivalent of M-Pesa: in Ghana, there is Tigo; in Côte d'Ivoire, there is Orange Money and Mobile Money from MTN (Mobile Telephone Network); in Nigeria, there is Glo Mobile from Globacom, Share Money, and many others; and the list could go on for each country in sub-Saharan Africa.

Creemers, Murugavel, Boutet, Omary, and Oikawa (2020) report:

> As African economies evolve, the mobile device will become the payment vehicle of first resort. … Africa's overall mobile financial services market penetration is currently second only to China's. … In Africa, for several reasons, telecom companies currently have a much higher market share in mobile payments than banks do.

In many countries, mobile or digital banking has become the solution of choice. As Nigel Green (2017) said several years ago with reference to Asia:

> Before our eyes we're seeing banking rapidly shift from buildings to smartphones. The days of visiting traditional banks are to become a distant memory in many parts of Asia. The physical activity of going into a bank to send a transfer, cash a check or report a stolen credit card are rapidly being replaced by an icon on a smartphone.

These changes in banking systems can be useful for local churches and mission agencies as banks seek to reduce their service fees by offering products that are better suited to their customers' needs. In addition, access to credit cards, or at least debit cards, will be of great service to church and mission leaders, not to mention the services provided to the missionaries themselves, although the mobile banking services operating through telecom companies may eliminate the need for such credit or debit cards in the future. Such user-friendly services will be much appreciated by users serving in God's mission field.

Another banking service that may be well suited to mission is savings accounts. Africa has a traditional savings system called a rotating savings and credit association, commonly called a *tontine* in French-speaking countries. In Ghana, this is called *susu*; in Ethiopia, *equb*; in Kenya, *chikola* or *harambee*; in Nigeria, *adashe*; and in Peru, *pandero*. Not only is this savings system more flexible than a savings account at the bank, but Abdoulaye Kane (2010, 174) states that "it should be noted that 92 percent of the *tontines* surveyed did not experience any serious failures."

This result is significantly better than most microfinance programs found at "modern" banks. Some of the latter have adapted their policies to this traditional system, resulting in the Grameen Bank in Bangladesh and the *tontibanques* in Cameroon, founded by Dr. Paul Fokam, who is also the founder of Afriland First Bank (Sembène 2015). It is interesting to note that the founder of a traditional bank has also been willing to adapt to include less traditional banking services.

Other adaptations of the *tontine* have been made by telecoms, such as Tigo in Ghana. Frédéric Maury of *Jeune Afrique* (2014, 15) explains:

Tigo has decided to offer an alternative to one of the most deeply rooted traditions in Ghana: susu, a very popular micro-credit program. The West African country thus has thousands of collectors to whom people, often women, entrust their savings. A system based on trust, which Tigo has decided to build on: since the beginning of 2013, subscribers can now save via Tigo. In six months, 6,000 women have decided to opt for this solution.

This adaptation resembles a personal micro-savings account, where each person can decide how much money they can deposit each time and how often they can take it out. It is likely that these conditions are prerequisites for opening such an account. Yet again, we see that flexibility rules in coming up with banking services adapted to meet the needs of the client.

Money Transfers

In addition to impacting commercial and economic power, information technology has also had a major impact on one specific area of mobile banking: that of money transfers. Such transfers can be used for paying utility bills, buying gasoline, or purchasing whatever product one wants via the e-commerce we've already discussed. But one major aspect of these transfers is known as P2P, referring to "person to person" transfers. In speaking of such mobile payments, Tijsbert Creemers et al. (2020) state that "The estimated potential market for banks in sub-Saharan Africa is $500 billion, nearly all of it in the form of person-to-person (P2P) payments."

Similar to the idea of remittances that we discussed earlier, such P2P payments can be a great boon to missionaries serving in Majority World countries. In fact, the day is already here in which donors can give their financial support directly to a missionary via their smartphone. This gives the donor assurance that the missionary will receive all of the contribution, since the sender usually pays the requisite fee for sending, if there is one.

The days may be numbered for the idea of sending funds to the mission agency, which then forwards the funds to the missionary on the field. Mission agencies that charge administrative fees on all financial support received in their office will have to find new ways to recoup those funds. And field missionaries will no longer have to wait weeks or months for their financial support to arrive. These new mobile banking procedures allow for almost immediate access to the funds, especially as telecommunication companies in various nations begin to partner with each other.

This new "cashless revolution" will have a great impact on local churches in the Majority World. First, a church can use mobile money services for its weekly collections, and congregants can contribute from their bank account—if they have one—or more likely, from their telephone accounts. This is a secure method for large churches that will no longer need to receive cash on site to support their ministries.

Second, local churches will also find it easier to support a mission agency or even a missionary family on the field—completing a simple and easy money transfer via a smartphone, as just discussed above.

At the same time, medical insurance or pension accounts can be more easily established for missionaries, as well as local church staff. In addition, fees for these services will surely decrease over time, which is another advantage for churches in Africa, Latin America, and Asia. This new technology is rapidly impacting church life and finances. It is impacting the church's role in world missions as well.

What About the Church?

The purpose of this section on the new economic position of the Majority World is to inform the reader of what is really happening today. Our traditional view of the Majority World being locked into near poverty needs to be adjusted. It is advancing by leaps and bounds in terms of economic and commercial growth; it is up to date in terms of mobile banking and money transfers; its projections for growth often surpass those of the more "modern" world; investments in Majority World countries are on the rise.

Questions of governance will need to be resolved, certainly, but that is also true for the Western world as well. A Majority World that is economically strong, that is well educated, and that has healthy children will be a force to be reckoned with. The business community believes in the Majority World and has already invested in such a vision. What about the church?

Chapter 10

A Pastor's Greatest Fear

In my research on new models of mission funding, some pastors expressed great concern about global mission. They asked, "If I encourage my church to focus on global mission, will this impoverish other ministries in the local church, including the pastor's salary?" This question is an important one, and that is why I sent a questionnaire that focuses on mission funding to churches in Asia and Africa. Nineteen churches responded to these questions—fourteen in Asia and five in Africa. Some churches responded in terms of actual amounts spent, while most responded in terms of percentages of their budget.

Among these nineteen local churches, the average mission budget was 44 percent of their overall church budget. For the few churches that gave their answers in actual amounts (three churches in Africa and one in Asia), their annual mission budget averaged more than $50,700 USD. Indeed, the other results coming from these churches would have been meaningless if their mission budget had been a very low figure. This shows that the churches that responded to the questionnaire are truly mission-minded churches.

Of course, it is one thing to set an extremely high mission budget and quite another to attain it. But among the churches surveyed, they financed on average 99.1 percent of what was budgeted for mission, or an average of 43.6 percent of the total church budget. For the few churches that gave their answers in actual amounts spent, their mission revenue averaged more than $51,300 USD per year, or 101.1 percent of the budgeted amount. These results indicate that these churches are very generous in their global mission allocations and that they are able to meet and even exceed their generous budgets. They are "putting their money where their mouth is."

I should point out that a fifth church that participated in my research gave its responses in actual amounts spent, but the results from this single denomination in West Africa would have skewed the averages to such a degree that their numbers were not included in these results. This one church alone had an annual mission budget of over $5,394,000 USD, and its mission revenue in 2016 alone exceeded $5,644,000 USD. You will therefore understand why these results were considered so exceptional that they were excluded from the averages. But that church denomination shows that extreme generosity toward world mission is possible even for a church in West Africa.

Another way to compare the mission budget to mission revenue was to see the number of churches for which revenue exceeded the budgeted amount. Two churches did not answer the question correctly, so their responses are not included in the average result. Only three of the remaining seventeen churches received less for mission than the amount that was in their mission budget; these three received an average of 84.7 percent of the budgeted amount. Seven of the seventeen churches received 100 percent of what was budgeted. Seven churches exceeded 100 percent of their mission budget, receiving an average of 117 percent of the mission budget. For those three churches that were unable to meet their mission budget, even though they were only able to contribute 84.7 percent of what was expected, this "bad" result seems quite positive for churches in the Majority World.

We now return to the fear expressed by some pastors. The questionnaire addressed this idea by asking three questions about the positive or negative impact of mission funding on the local church. A large majority of respondents (83 percent) said that their focus on mission had *not* prevented the payment of salaries for church staff, and that same majority (83 percent) said that their focus on mission has not prevented the funding of other ministries. These results should be welcome news to a large number of pastors, as they suggest that their fears about mission are unfounded. In other words, roughly five out of six churches that focus on mission are not negatively affected in terms of funding for local ministries or the pastor's salary. Of course, a pastor might say that he could be that sixth person who would be negatively affected, but the odds are on his side. These results confirm what others say about the impact of mission on the local church: "All the studies show that faith-promise missions giving actually *enhances other church giving*, especially regular budget giving" (Christian Reformed World Missions, n.d., 2, emphasis mine).

One pastor in Abuja, Nigeria, Dr. Azaki Nash, encouraged his church to increase the number of missionaries they supported from 100 to 125. He relates (*AfriGo* June 2022, 5) that he had to convince his leaders to *not* increase his own financial support, but to give the increased giving to the missionaries.

> Every pastor who will be effective in promoting missions must divest personal interests away, even when the leadership team is reluctant to spend more on the missionary than on their pastor. These are some bottlenecks I had to overcome in sending 25 more missionaries.

Returning to the questionnaire, a majority similar to the previous one (81 percent) responded that their focus on mission funding actually *helped* to promote funding from other departments. Roughly four out of five pastors said that the focus on mission has not only *not* decreased church finances, but it has actually *improved* the financial situation of their churches.

Finally, here is a comparison of responses from mission-minded churches in Africa with their counterparts in Asia, noting however that a sample size of five African churches and fourteen Asian churches is not very representative. Therefore, while these results are interesting, they cannot be considered statistically valid.

In percentage terms, the average mission budget for mission-minded churches in Africa was 10.8 percent of the total local church budget, while the average mission budget for such churches in Asia was 46.7 percent. In terms of amounts received for mission, African churches received an average of 12.7 percent of the total mission budget, an excess of 1.9 percent over the budgeted amount. On the other hand, Asian churches received 45.5 percent of the total budget, a deficit of 1.2 percent compared to the amount budgeted. So churches in Africa tend to put a relatively small amount into the church's mission budget, but they slightly exceed it (117.3 percent) through their contributions. Churches in Asia tend to set a very generous mission budget, but they don't quite (97.6 percent) meet it.

In terms of the impact of mission on local church funding, all five of the African churches said that their missionary focus had not diminished church funding, neither for church staff salaries nor for local ministries. For the fourteen churches in Asia, about three-fourths of the churches also said that their focus on mission had not had a negative financial impact on the local church. For those churches that said that their mission focus had actually helped their financial situation, there was almost no difference between the two groups; 80 percent of churches in Africa and 82 percent of churches in Asia said their mission focus had a positive impact on their local revenue.

My overall conclusion is that a pastor's fear of a negative financial impact on local ministries or on his own salary because of an emphasis on mission is not justified. Although this research is far from exhaustive, it is consistent with the conclusions drawn by others on the impact of mission funding, such as Christian Reformed World Missions. This research also indicates that there are churches that are capable of great generosity in the Majority World, including Africa. So let us move forward with courage and faith regarding global mission funding.

Chapter 11

So What?

In light of all that has been shared up to this point, a local church pastor or member can still ask, "So what?" To answer that question, I give the following recommendations for mission funding by evangelical churches in the Majority World. My hope is that churches and mission agencies in Asia, Latin America, Eastern Europe, and Africa will begin to implement these recommendations and see for themselves the amazing impact for Jesus Christ they can have in faraway places. I also hope that churches and mission agencies in Western Europe, North America and Oceania will learn from the models that many Majority World churches are implementing.

1) Mission agencies and local churches in the Majority World should break out of the traditional model of mission funding and make use of the many other funding models that are available to them. Both the literature and my research

have shown that many of these models are acceptable to pastors and mission leaders and are already being practiced in many Majority World countries.

2) Missionary funding should not be the sole responsibility of the missionary. The traditional model has its strengths, especially in terms of a better relationship with donors and their prayer for the missionary. But financially, it is based on certain realities that do not apply to the Majority World, such as a fairly high economic level, a nuclear family that provides some financial stability, disposable income in the missionary's home country, an acceptance of approaching potential donors to ask for money for oneself, and a history that is based on a business model. All of these factors are quite foreign to many Majority World cultures, as missionary leaders in Argentina and Ethiopia have noted earlier.

3) Local churches should focus on a mission vision without fear of lacking resources for missionary funding. My research (Welch 2019) shows that the vast majority of churches that engage in significant mission efforts have no financial difficulties afterward. In fact, these churches are in a better financial position after their commitment to world mission. Several pastors and mission leaders in Ethiopia have confirmed that there is no shortage of resources in the Majority World. Juanita, the Peruvian missionary who went to Thailand (mentioned in chapter 5) insisted that yes, fundraising can be done in Latin America even in these difficult and uncertain times. Resources are not lacking. Rather, it is a mission vision that is most lacking.

4) Each local church would benefit greatly by forming a Mission Start-up Group (MSG) to promote global mission among church members. This group can mobilize not only mission funds but also interest in and prayer for missionaries and unreached people groups. Such a group can also greatly assist families returning from the mission field. If a local church supports several missionaries, each one should have a representative—a third party—who is a member of this mission start-up group.

5) In funding models where a salary is already provided, these situations should be used especially for missionaries who want to work in countries that don't formally accept missionaries. These models include the tentmaking missionary, the business-as-mission model (BAM), and the missionary who is a professional worker (teacher, doctor, engineer, etc.). The model where the missionary is a salaried employee of his or her home church should not be used for these countries, even if the salary is already provided, since it is difficult to hide the "paper trail" for such a salary. But if a salary comes from a non-church or non-mission entity, this can safeguard the professional "worker" and allow him or her to work longer abroad.

6) Local churches should take advantage of businessmen/women to train missionaries who must go to the foreign mission field as professional "workers" instead of as formal "missionaries." Too many churches see these businessmen/women as a "bank account" to finance church programs, neglecting their gifts and talents to train those who go out on mission. This training is critical for missionaries who adopt the BAM model. Such training could even create a heart for mission among these businessmen/women, and the church could at the same time provide missiological training for them.

7) A tentmaking missionary should choose a job and an employer that is credible to the local population, and their work should be in a field where they can excel. Preferably, the missionary should not hold a position that a local person could hold, so as not to be looked down upon by others. As much as possible, they should also strive to make sure that adequate working conditions are maintained for themselves and their colleagues.

8) Local churches should be prepared to use nontraditional approaches to mission funding. This could include the twelve-church model, where each local church provides missionary support for one month each year, as was the case in Bolivia. Another nontraditional model is the "handful of rice" model, as used in India, which is proving very effective even in poorer parts of the world. These approaches are proof that churches around the world have been quite creative in their mission funding.

9) Local churches can also benefit from revolving savings plans, which are more a method to be used with other models than a model in and of itself. This method is, in fact, very traditional instead of nontraditional, since it exists almost everywhere in the Majority World. Some local churches in Ethiopia have already used it for mission funding, according to my research. Local churches could put a revolving savings plan into practice and do so to save money for mission. If a certain amount or percentage of money was taken immediately from the offering each week and put into a separate account designated for mission, local churches would see to what extent it is possible—even quite easy—to raise money for mission. This traditional practice, like its more modern banking adaptation, certainly lends itself to mission funding.

10) Mission agencies can and should accommodate these different models of mission financing. This means that administrative rules and policies should be flexible and preferably simple. These agencies need to review the conditions for becoming a "member" of the mission and what this means financially. They must be willing to cooperate with employers and vice versa and sign memoranda of understanding with these "workers."

11) Mission agencies should also be ready to participate in the financial support of their missionaries, especially with regard to the administrative side. A mission in northeast India seeks funding for all administrative matters: medical insurance, life insurance, retirement, visa and work permit fees, etc. (Welch 2019). As one person in Ethiopia said, local churches do not understand this administrative side well, since most church members don't benefit from these things themselves. Therefore, mission agencies should seek to finance this "incomprehensible" part of the monthly budget themselves instead of asking the missionary to do so.

12) Local churches in the Majority World should decide to do regular projects and activities as a means of mission funding. Such projects and activities may cause a local church to put a "mission" line item in the church budget which, more than anything else, shows that the church takes global mission seriously. This demonstrates that mission is not a subsidiary or optional activity for the local church. Many examples were discovered and have been cited in this research.

13) It is crucial that local churches and mission agencies take the African examples in the Bible seriously and follow them. In the book of Acts, there were Africans who were present at the birth of the church, at the birth of cross-cultural mission, and, one could argue, at the birth of missionary training in the church. From the very beginning of the mission, Africans were involved. It is time for the Majority World church, represented by the church in Africa in Scripture, to rekindle this same enthusiasm for mission.

14) Mission agencies and local churches can follow the example of the global business sector and believe in the economic future of the Majority World. Evidence surrounds us with regard to economic advances, the enormous investments being made, new developments in the world of information, the new link between smartphones and banking, advances in the private sector, and the growing number of competent entrepreneurs. Progress is undeniable, and the economic future of the Majority World is very promising.

15) The Majority World church should reflect on how it can use smartphones for mission. The use of smartphones means that the local church can stay in direct contact with its missionary on another continent. The pastor of a home church can pray in real time with their missionaries on the field. A missionary can take theological refresher courses without returning home. A missionary family can easily talk to parents and see them on screens for holidays and birthdays. Financial donors can transfer money directly to the missionary abroad. The list could go on and on. Advances in

telephone technology are a boon to the church in Africa, Asia, and Latin America, if only the church would take time to reflect on a more effective utilization of this tool.

These recommendations can help the Majority World church take a much more active part in global mission, a part that is not modelled on what Western churches and mission agencies are doing. The Majority World church increasingly understands that every church in the world, not just churches in the Western world or the few "rich" churches in Asia, is expected to participate in global mission. Each has its part to play and each has a unique contribution to offer, for the church of Jesus Christ is, indeed, an interdependent church. International mission teams better represent the universal gospel than do monocultural mission teams.

A "one size fits all" model of mission funding is no longer appropriate in our world. Because churches and countries that send missionaries are so different from one another, funding models for sending missionaries must be different from each other as well. A wide variety of sending countries requires a wide variety of funding models. Our God is both Creator and creative. New mission funding models should follow his example.

Appendix

Africa's New Economic Standing

While the objective of this book is to relate to churches all across the Majority World in the area of missionary funding, a great deal of my research, along with thirty-one years of my life, pertains to Africa. And unlike Asia and Latin America, Africa has been perceived as a continent with so many economic problems that it will always be playing "catch up" in regard to sending out missionaries. But I would like to say that such a perception is wrong. For not only has the Christian church made tremendous strides forward in the last half-century, but so has the African economy.

Just like in Asia, Latin America, and Eastern Europe, there are countries in Africa that have known significant social and economic progress and those that have known political and technological setbacks. And those that have known technological and economic progress, but social and political setbacks. You can arrange those adjectives around those two nouns however you want and find a country in Africa, Asia, Latin America, or Eastern Europe where they will be accurate. And unfortunately, the same can be increasingly applied to Western Europe and North America.

In so many ways, Africa is not all that different from any other continent on this planet (with the exception of Antarctica). But old ways of seeing Africa die hard. That is why I would like to add this appendix.

It is true that African countries face considerable obstacles to their economies: insufficient infrastructure, very low levels of banking, poorly developed industries, high unemployment, and many others. According to Luca Ventura (2022) in the economic journal *Global Finance*, out of 192 countries, the twelve poorest countries in the world, based on GDP per capita, are all in Africa. Burundi occupies the unfortunate first place on the list. Moreover, of the forty poorest countries in the world, thirty-one are in Africa. Outside of Africa, Yemen comes in the lowest at number 180.

On the other hand, among the richest countries in the world, the first African country on this list is the Seychelles, which is the fifty-seventh richest country in the world, just before Malaysia (number fifty-eight). Africa's "giants" in terms of population are barely among the top one hundred richest countries: South Africa occupies place number ninety-nine, and the others are not among the top hundred; Egypt numbers 101, Nigeria occupies place number 144, Ethiopia number 161, and the Democratic Republic of the Congo number 189, nine places after Yemen!

How is it, then, that Nigeria sends thousands of missionaries around the world? How is it that Ethiopia sends missionaries to Pakistan and China? Logically, their lower economic rank should prevent them from sending so many missionaries abroad. Apparently rank on the list of poor countries is not the only clue to consider. Here are some other economic observations regarding the African continent.

Economic Growth

Certain attitudes toward Africa during the twentieth century are no longer valid in the twenty-first century, since the situation has changed, especially economically. In the *African Business Journal*, Mohamadou Sy (2013, 34–35) writes:

> Trade between Africa and the rest of the world has increased by 200% since 2000. Intra-African trade has jumped from 6% to 13% of the total volume since 2000. However, the continent directs only 13% of its exports to itself,

compared to 50% for Asia and 70% for Europe. Inflation plunged from 22% in the 1990s to 8% in the past decade. External debt declined by a quarter and budget deficits by two-thirds. In addition to its resilience to the crisis, the nature of the continent's growth is surprising, and this time it seems to be supported by strong domestic demand.

This kind of remark can be found almost everywhere in articles and books that talk about the African economy today. In their book *The Next Africa*, Jake Bright and Aubrey Hruby (2015, 47) explain that:

> Since 2000, FDI in Sub-Saharan Africa has increased seven times, more than doubling between 2004 ($12 billion) and 2008 ($38 billion) and increasing by 42 percent from 2008 to 2014 to $55 billion.

Even *The Economist* magazine, which in 2000 gave Africa the notorious label of "the hopeless continent" (Bright and Hruby 2015, 7), reported in January 2011 that "among the ten fastest growing economies in the decade 2000–2010, Africa had six. It argued that by 2015, the African continent would produce seven of the top ten economies" (Bright and Hruby 2015, 21). Today's Africa is convincing yesterday's sceptics.

Investments

France invests in the countries that are part of its former colonies, but not with a sense of historical obligation. The journalist Hichem Ben Yaïche (2016, 21) interviewed Xavier Beulin, the president of the French food group Avril. The latter explained that

> agriculture is part of a political strategy. It is no longer I who say this, it is the great international observers. That's why we, today, believe in the African continent. ... There are groups like Avril—and there are others, including Bolloré, which is doing things in its field—who believe in Africa, and who are ready to invest. ... Finally, the continent that, in my view, will develop in the coming decades is Africa. So we'd better go there.

It is very clear that the commercial world sees Africa with a new perspective compared to the past, and the "great international observers" Beulin spoke of confirm this.

A 2014 survey coordinated by South African associations indicated that a majority (70 percent) of private equity firms prefer to invest in Africa compared to other major world regions because of its relatively high growth rate compared to other regions of the world (Jones 2014). An earlier survey by a Washington-based private equity association found a similar result, with 54 percent of fund managers planning to start or continue investing in Africa (Jones 2014).

The president and CEO of a private equity firm in the United States, Elizabeth Littlefield (2014), explains that researchers found that investment in Africa yielded an annual return of 11.2 percent, which is better than US venture capital funds. Specifically, FDI in sub-Saharan Africa has shown a growth rate of 19.5 percent over the past seven years (Littlefield, 2014). Such results explain why international donors see Africa as a very promising and attractive place to invest.

In an issue of *African Business* magazine that focuses on the economic relationship between Africa and Singapore, the CEO of the Greater Kingdom consulting firm, Stephen Bwansa, says: "There is an abundance of opportunity in Africa. These are the same opportunities that China offered forty years ago" (Ford 2015, 8). The chairman of that firm's board of directors, Elim Chew, adds: "Africa is the next frontier. It is a huge market and needs what Singapore offers" (Ford 2015, 8).

These quotes clearly show that Asian countries are ready to invest in Africa, and it is not only Singapore that is doing so. According to journalist Sébastien Le Belzic, "Since 2009, China has been Africa's largest trading partner. … In the last ten years, China has invested more than $75 billion, almost as much as the United States" (Le Belzic 2016, 28). However, other experts report that Malaysia's total investment portfolio in Africa exceeds that of China's (Bright & Hruby, 2015). And my personal experience in Côte d'Ivoire shows that other Asian countries, especially those in the Middle East, such as Iran, Turkey, and Saudi Arabia, are ready to invest in the banking and infrastructure sectors. Donors from around the world are now looking to Africa, a continent that is worth the risk.

Remittances

An additional element worth mentioning here is the money sent to Africa by what is known as the African Diaspora—that is, Africans who have immigrated to countries outside the African continent. It is common knowledge that Africans are very generous, and those who leave their home countries to find work in Europe, North America, or Asia send money regularly to their families who stay in Africa. But the size of these remittances is often not published.

Bright and Hruby inform us that since 2010, the money sent by electronic transfer to sub-Saharan Africa exceeds the amount that this region receives in foreign aid. And in the two years 2010 and 2011 for the entire continent, they report that remittances from African immigrants exceeded FDI for the continent (Bright & Hruby, 2015). Figures for 2015 indicate that remittances by members of the African Diaspora reached $62 billion, while FDIs amount to $55 billion and foreign aid for Africa amounts to $50 billion (Fiano, 2017).

This African generosity by those in the diaspora is something the African church should take into account. There are undoubtedly many Christians in the African Diaspora who would be very open to programs and projects that advance the kingdom of God through African missionaries.

Risks

Despite all these examples of economic growth in Africa and the many cases of investment in Africa, does this mean that there are no longer any financial problems on the African continent? Of course not. These same authors, journalists, and investors recognize that problems still exist. Bright and Hruby (2015, 112) explain:

> We see three causes of disruption that could hinder the revolutionary economic advances of some African countries: massive unemployment and public discord; institutional inability to align the motivations of the hyper-rich with the common good; rare and unexpected changes in the market.

Bright and Hruby understand that a number of good statistics don't mean that everything is rosy. There are still obstacles to overcome. Other observers agree. Mohamadou Sy (2013, 40) notes that the governance problem is still there:

> Africa is making little progress in building states governed by the rule of law, based on free and transparent elections where citizens participate peacefully in the political life of their country. While the number of authoritarian regimes remains stable, the number of hybrid (or semi-democratic) regimes and imperfect democracies is increasing very slightly.

Neil Ford states that political, economic, and security instabilities have deterred some Singaporean companies from investing in the past and quotes a director of International Enterprise in Singapore who says that "pockets of unrest" may exist (Ford 2015, 8). These remarks show that the negative side of Africa has not yet disappeared, and even that there is still much progress to be made. Even groups that facilitate investment in Africa talk on the one hand about FDI, which has increased from $566 million in 2003 to over $6 billion in 2013, and then, on the other hand, they talk about the legal, economic, political, and operational problems ravaging the African continent (Songhai Advisory Limited Loability Partnership, n.d.).

At the same time, however, all these remarks indicate that Africa has made progress economically in recent years and is likely to continue to do so. With stronger economies and increasing investment, the number of jobs will increase, development will progress, and economic and financial opportunities for employees will grow. The business community already seems to recognize Africa as a continent with great financial promise. Its vision for Africa is almost limitless.

All of the examples cited are essentially about the financial side of the economy in modern Africa. But there are many other aspects that make the African economy much more developed than in the past, and thus they should not be treated in the same way. We will now look at some of these aspects, but we will not go into them in great detail.

Telecommunications

The sector that is probably the most impressive is the telecommunications sector. With the advent of cellular phones, telephones in Africa have jumped over many generations of technology at once. According to Bright and Hruby (2015), about 70 percent of Africans south of the Sahara own a cell phone. Based on our own experience in urban Abidjan, we estimate that in the city the percentage of people owning a cell phone is close to 90 percent of the population. And this is only the beginning, as "smartphones," which are much more powerful than the first cell phones, are starting to gain more market share.

Bright and Hruby (2015, 187–88) state:

> Africa's conversion to smartphones and other Internet devices will present more than one global opportunity for telephone companies. It will completely transform business and social activity on the continent, especially with the improvement of broadband. Smartphones will become the central platform for almost everything in Africa.

One might wonder if this idea, published in 2015, has not already been attained. With a smartphone, customers can buy fuel at a gas station. With a smartphone they can pay their electricity bill. With a smartphone they can transfer money to someone else; they can receive video messages from their friends; they can participate in a training course from another continent while driving down a highway in Africa; they can receive a warning about an unsafe incident that is taking place in a certain area of their city; they can order an evening meal and have it delivered to their home; they can reserve and purchase an airline ticket and receive the boarding pass. This list could go on and on.

In 2016 the major telephone company Orange entered into a new partnership with the cyber giant Google for the African and Middle Eastern markets. They announced that "this partnership will make it possible to offer customers the best of both partners in terms of access and content, through an all-inclusive digital communication package" (Choisnet 2016, 6). This means that in the future, people will be able to do even more with their smartphones, and at a lower price.

Information Technology

Advances in the field of telephone technology owe their success to another sector of the economy, that of information technology. Information technology is better known by the abbreviation IT. Without information technology, communication would never have had the opportunity to benefit from these advances.

Many information start-ups exist in East Africa, especially in Kenya, which has acquired the name "Silicon Savannah" (taken from the name "Silicon Valley" in California where many small information companies are located). These small information companies use technology in smartphones to enable a person to do anything they can imagine. For example, a farmer can put small chips in the ears of his cows or goats to track not only the movement of his herds, but also the health of each animal. Or a city dweller can use his smartphone to avoid traffic jams on his way home from work. More and more people are buying their household items or clothes on the Jumia platform, which also provides home delivery.

In 2016 Jumia, under the supervision of AIG in Nigeria, announced a partnership with Axa, "enabling the French group to become the exclusive provider of insurance products and services on the Jumia platform as well as on all of AIG's other online and mobile platforms" (Choisnet 2016, 6). This list could be continued ad infinitum. But two things should be emphasized. On the one hand, these new information technology companies can be found almost everywhere now in Africa, just as in other parts of the Majority World. Bright and Hruby (2015) believe that this is due to the energetic influence of small information technology companies in the Silicon Savannah. Since this phenomenon is catching on worldwide, it is difficult to truly know the real motivation behind all these start-ups.

On the other hand, we must emphasize the impact of this new technological wave on money transfers. For example, in Kenya, the major telecommunications company, Safaricom, has initiated the M-Pesa service— the letter M stands for "mobile" and *pesa* is the Swahili word for "money." Within two years, M-Pesa had more than six million customers and was transferring more than $1.5 billion each year (Bright and Hruby 2015). This new method of money transfer greatly increases security for merchants, who no longer have to carry a lot of cash on their person. It helps parents pay their children's school fees more easily.

The equivalent of one-third of Kenya's GDP goes through M-Pesa, making Kenya one of the most advanced countries in terms of a non-monetary economy (Bright and Hruby 2015). And many countries have their equivalent to M-Pesa: in Ghana there is Tigo; in Côte d'Ivoire there is Orange Money and Mobile Money from MTN; in Nigeria there is Glo Mobile from Globacom, Share Money, and many others; and the list could go on for each country in sub-Saharan Africa.

This new cashless revolution will have a great impact on local churches in the Majority World. First, a church can use mobile money services for its weekly offerings, and congregants can contribute from their bank accounts—if they have one—or telephone accounts. This is a secure method for large churches that will no longer need to receive cash on site to support their ministries. Second, local churches will also find it easier to support a mission agency or even a missionary family on the field, completing a simple and easy money transfer via a smartphone.

At the same time, medical insurance or pension accounts can be more easily established for missionaries as well as local church staff. In addition, fees for these services will surely decrease over time, which is another advantage for the church in Africa, Latin America, and Asia. This new technology is rapidly impacting church life and finances.

Banking

Another sector mentioned in an earlier chapter is banking. In the Majority World, this sector works very well in Asian countries and quite well in most countries in Latin America. But in Africa, the situation is different. With regard to traditional banking before the advent of new technologies, about 80 percent of Africans did not have access to traditional banking (Fiano 2017), due to a lack of secure wages or land that could be used as collateral. As a result, there is a huge customer base that banks can still attract, and increasingly the "mobile bank" is providing the convenient services desired by its customers. According to Hichem Ben Yaïche and Guillaume Weill-Raynal (2016, 14), Boubker Jaï, the general manager of Attijariwafa Bank, says:

> Moreover, the challenge for us, everywhere on the continent, is to be in perfect coherence with local needs. It is not only a question of duplicating products that have worked elsewhere, but above all, of understanding the market well and proposing adapted products. In terms of functionality, of course, but also in terms of price.

This quote shows that banks are looking to adapt to the real needs of their customers and to do so at an affordable price. These changes can be useful for local churches and mission agencies as banks seek to reduce their service fees by offering products that are better suited to their customers' needs. In addition, access to credit cards, or at least debit cards, will be of great service to church and mission leaders, not to mention the services provided to the missionaries themselves. Such user-friendly services will be much appreciated by users serving in God's mission field.

Another banking service that may be well suited to mission is savings accounts. Africa has a traditional savings system called a rotating savings and credit association, commonly called a *tontine* in French-speaking countries. In Ghana, it is called *susu*; in Ethiopia, *equb*; in Kenya, *chikola*, or *harambee*; in Nigeria, *adashe*; and in Peru, *pandero*. Not only is this savings system more flexible than a savings account at the bank, but Abdoulaye Kane states that "it should be noted that 92 percent of the *tontines* surveyed did not experience any serious failures" (Kane 2010, 174). This result is significantly better than most microfinance programs found at "modern" banks. Some of the latter have adapted their policies to this traditional system, resulting in the Grameen Bank in Bangladesh or the *tontibanques* in Cameroon, founded by Dr. Paul Fokam, who is also the founder of Afriland First Bank (Sembène 2015). Other adaptations of the *tontine* have been made by telecoms, such as Tigo in Ghana. Frédéric Maury of *Jeune Afrique* (2014, 15) explains:

> Tigo has decided to offer an alternative to one of the most deeply rooted traditions in Ghana: susu, a very popular micro-credit program. The West African country thus has thousands of collectors to whom people, often women, entrust their savings. A system based on trust, which Tigo has decided to build on: since the beginning of 2013, subscribers can now save via Tigo. In six months, 6,000 women would have decided to opt for this solution.

This adaptation resembles a personal *tontine*, where each person can decide how much money they can deposit each time and how often they can take it out. It is likely that these conditions are prerequisites for opening such an account.

Governance

Another very important sector is the government sector. Some countries in the Majority World are known for their deficiencies in good governance, despite quite a few exceptions to this "rule" and enormous efforts being made in this sector. In the magazine *African Business*, the journalist Yacouba Barma Aboubacar (2016, 32) acknowledges "that several encouraging developments are already at work: more and more states are adopting sectoral visions structured and materialized by quantified plans and targeted investment projects in all areas." This shows that government ministers take their work seriously, which gives confidence to economic operators.

There was also the creation in 2008 of the Tony Blair Africa Governance Initiative, established by the former Prime Minister of the United Kingdom. This program is supposed to equip African leaders with the capacity to deliver more effective public services to their citizens. In addition, it aims at collaboration between the private sector and government officials in order to tackle poverty. In 2011 the major Nigerian entrepreneur, Tony Elumelu, former CEO of United Bank of Africa (UBA), joined Blair to develop expertise and capacity at the center of government to improve the business climate in these countries (Africa Governance Initiative, 2011).

These efforts also seek to end government corruption, which can only benefit society at large, including churches and mission agencies. Effective administration, a legal system that is fair, education where promotion is based on merit, well-developed and modern infrastructure, efficient public health, and appointments to government positions free of patronage—all of these characterize a well-functioning government sector.

Moreover, the population of each country should be able to benefit from all these elements. Local churches should lead the fight for these improvements because, in doing so, they will be demonstrating holistic ministries that will reach out to the whole of African society and, in turn, open doors for Africans in Africa and around the world. All of the logistics of sending African missionaries will be simplified if African governments function effectively.

What About the Church?

The purpose of this section on the economic position of the Majority World, and especially of Africa, is to inform the reader of what is really happening with all these statistics and quotations that concern the world today, not to mention the Africa of 2050 when it will represent 40 percent of the world's population instead of 15 percent, as it does currently. Africa's population is expected to reach one billion by then, surpassing China and India if birth trends continue at the current rate (Bright and Hruby, 2015).

This fact in and of itself will give Africa a powerful position in the world. But an Africa that is economically strong and politically stable will be even more powerful. The same is true of an Africa that has strong infrastructure, well-educated citizens, and healthy children. Africa is already moving toward these goals. The business community believes in Africa and has already invested in this vision. What about the church?

Acknowledgments

A book is always a collaborative effort, and this one is no exception. The idea for this particular book came in 2013, when SIM asked me to chair its "New Sending Entities" task force. Our goal was to identify the financial challenges being faced by churches in various countries that wanted to send out their own missionaries. I am grateful for the privilege I had to work with Jared Oginga (Kenya), Watson Rajaratnam (Singapore), Julieta Murillo (Ecuador) and Siegfried Ngubane (South Africa) on that task force.

Our work together motivated me all the more to continue my own work on a just-begun doctorate. So I want to thank my SIM supervisor at that time, Dave Bremner (South Africa) for granting me permission to begin my doctoral studies while still being a full-time missionary in West Africa. And I need to especially thank Worku Hailemariam, director of the SIM East Africa Office in Addis Ababa, for the invaluable help he gave me when I was in Ethiopia, interviewing mission leaders whose comments were most insightful. With no prompting from me, Worku set up and then drove me to those interviews which made my findings far more interesting and pertinent than he will ever realize.

I also want to thank Martine Audéoud and Glenn Smith, without whose support my dissertation would have been either a non-starter or a non-finished work.

Let me add a surprising acknowledgement here. Since an inanimate entity cannot receive my gratitude, I want to thank the creators of the website DeepL for the amazingly accurate work it did in translating my original French dissertation into English. While obviously there were corrections to be made afterward, DeepL simplified my task by translating huge amounts of text both quickly and with surprising accuracy. For that I am most grateful.

I must also note that working with the team at William Carey Publishing has been a joy. By the grace of God I met Vivian Doub at a large conference in Hungary, and she was the first person to show an interest in publishing this book. She was not the first publisher I spoke to, by the way, but she was the first one to show an interest. Thank you, Vivian, for getting the ball rolling. Denise Wynn and Melissa Hicks have provided advice and encouragement all along the way. And what can I say about the cover? Without the artistic expertise of Mike Riester, this book would never have had such a beautiful cover. Thank you, Mike, Denise, and others who collaborated to make the cover so attractive.

It may sound unusual to refer to a copy editor/proofreader as "courageous," but that was my conclusion after looking at all the editorial changes that Andrew Sloan proposed. Not only did he improve the text ("activating" all my passives, for example), but he was not afraid to also challenge some of my ideas in terms of both word choice and the underlying theology of those words. As a result I had to make a number of changes, and I even had to delete one paragraph because in the end I concluded it wasn't doctrinally sound. And for years I had thought it was. Thank you, Andrew, for your excellent attention to detail and your valuable contribution to the overall concepts presented in this book. You have improved it beyond measure.

Let me also thank Joshua Bogunjoko, the SIM International Director, for asking me to share these ideas at the SIM African Mobilization Consultation in June 2023, and for giving copies of this book to each participant. It is always encouraging to authors when their book is put into the hands of those who can implement its ideas.

Of course, a book takes time to write, which meant my wife Janet had to sacrifice time with her husband, both physically and emotionally. Even though she's getting used to that idea, I cannot thank her enough for the fabulous support she always gives me during such endeavors. Thank you, lady of my life.

And I must say a giant "thank you" to our Lord Jesus Christ, who has been so obviously active in this whole book-writing process: having mission leaders ask me to undertake this task in the first place; helping me find a publisher while in a faraway country; orchestrating events to get endorsements from some people who don't even know me but still agreed to read and then recommend this book; coordinating the timing of a mobilization consultation with the printing of this book. The hand of the Lord has been with all of us throughout this whole process. For that, and to him, I am most grateful.

Reference List

Aboubacar, Yacouba B. 2016. "Des solutions africaines aux défis africains." *African Business* [French edition] 43: 31–33.

Africa Governance Initiative. 2011. "The Blair Elumelu Fellowship Programme: Supporting African Governments to Advance Economic Development." Press release. AllAfrica InfoWire. https://allafrica.com/stories/201106151336.html.

AfriGo. 2022. "The Pastor: A Crucial Advocate for Missions." Azaki Nash 7, no. 2 (June): 5.

AfriGo. 2022. "A Pastor's Heart, A Church's Response." Azaki Nash 7, no. 2 (June): 7.

Anderson, Courtney. 1987. *To the Golden Shore: The Life of Adoniram Judson.* Valley Forge, PA: Judson Press.

Bakke, Dennis W. 2005. *Joy at Work: A Revolutionary Approach to Fun on the Job.* Seattle: PVG.

Barber, Ben. 2018. "Authoritarianism Gains in Southeast Asia." *The Foreign Service Journal.* https://afsa.org/authoritarianism-gains-southeast-asia.

Ben Yaïche, Hichem. 2016. "L'Afrique, il faut y aller." *African Business* [French edition] 43: 18–21.

Ben Yaïche, Hichem, and Guillaume Weill-Raynal. 2016. "Nous offrons les synergies d'un groupe régional." *African Business* [French edition] 43: 14–17.

Bessenecker, Scott. 2014a. *Overturning Tables: Freeing Missions from the Christian-Industrial Complex.* Downers Grove, IL: InterVarsity Press.

Bessenecker, Scott. 2014b. "Turning the White Parachurch Ship Around?—A Solutions Guest Post," by Scott Bessenecker. *Minister Different—Series: Funding Multiethnic Mission.*

Bjork, David. 2015. *Nous sommes tous disciples!* Carlisle, UK: Langham Global Library.

Blomberg, Craig. 2013. *Christians in an Age of Wealth: A Biblical Theology of Stewardship.* Grand Rapids, MI: Zondervan.

Bonk, Jonathan. 2006. *Missions and Money.* Revised and expanded. Maryknoll, NY: Orbis Books, 2006.

Borthwick, Paul. 2012. *Western Christians in Global Mission: What's the Role of the North American Church?* Downers Grove, IL: InterVarsity Press.

Bright, Jake, and Aubrey Hruby. 2015. *The Next Africa: An Emerging Continent Becomes a Global Powerhouse.* New York: St. Martin's Press.

Bureau of Economic Analysis (BEA). 2022a. "Gross Domestic Product, Second Quarter 2022 (Advance Estimate)." https://www.bea.gov/news/2022/gross-domestic-product-second-quarter-2022-advance-estimate.

Bureau of Economic Analysis (BEA). 2022b. Table 1. "Direct Investment Abroad: Selected Items by Country of Foreign Affiliate, 2018–21." https://www.bea.gov/data/intl-trade-investment/direct-investment-country-and-industry.

Bush, Luis. 1990. *Funding Third World Missions: The Pursuit of True Christian Partnership*. Singapore/Wheaton, IL: World Evangelical Fellowship Missions Commission.

"Business as Mission: The Effective Use of Tentmaking in North Africa." 2011. Anonymous dissertation Southern Baptist Theological Seminary.

Chevalier, Stephanie. 2022. "Leading Online Marketplaces in Latin America in 2021, by Monthly Visits." https://www.statista.com/statistics/321543/latin-america-online-retailer-visitors/.

Christian Reformed World Missions. *Faith Promise Giving*. Grand Rapids: Christian Reformed World Missions, n.d.

Choisnet, Gérard. 2016. "Orange et Google s'associent dans l'Internet mobile." *African Business* [French edition] 43: 6.

Choisnet, Gérard. 2016. "AXA s'installe sur la plateforme Jumia." *African Business* [French edition] 43: 6.

Clark, D. 2022. "GDP Growth Rate Forecasts in Europe 2022." https://www.statista.com/statistics/1102546/coronavirus-european-gdp-growth/.

Clark, Dennis. 1971. *The Third World and Mission*. Waco, TX: Word Books.

Clines, David E. 2006. "The Mobilization of Honduran Baptists to Fulfill the Great Commission through the Creation of an Indigenous Sending Agency." Dissertation, Gordon-Conwell Theological Seminary.

Collins, Tom. 2022. "Economic Outlook 2022: Africa Faces Rickety Rebound." *African Business*. (January) https://african.business/2022/01/trade-investment/economic-outlook-2022-africa-faces-rickety-rebound/.

Creemers, Tijsbert, Thiruneeran Murugavel, Frédéric Boutet, Othman Omary, and Takeshi Oikawa. 2020. "Five Strategies for Mobile-Payment Banking in Africa." Boston Consulting Group. https://www.bcg.com/publications/2020/five-strategies-for-mobile-payment-banking-in-africa.

Danker, William J. 2002. *Profit for the Lord: Economic Activities in Moravian Missions and the Basel Mission Trading Company*. Eugene, OR: Wipf and Stock.

Didache. http://www.thedidache.com. n.d.

Doyle, C. Andrew. 2015. *A Generous Community: Being the Church in a New Missionary Age*. New York: Morehouse Publishing.

Emets, Yana. 2017. "9 Technological Innovations from Africa." *The Borgen Project* (blog). https://borgenproject.org/africa-technology-innovations/.

Escobar, Samuel. 2003. *A Time for Mission: The Challenge for Global Christianity*. Nottingham, UK: InterVarsity Press.

Ezemadu, Reuben. 2005. *Sending and Supporting African Missionaries in the 21st Century*. Ibadan, Nigeria: ACCLAIM.

Fiano, Andrea. 2017. "Africa 2017: The Future of Banking Everywhere." *Global Finance*. (October) https://www.gfmag.com/magazine/october-2017/africa-2017-future-banking-everywhere.

Ford, Neil. 2015. "From Singapore to the World." *African Business* 420: 6–9.

Galvan, Hector. 2021. "A Guide to Payment Methods in Latin America." Redbridge. https://www.redbridgedta.com/us/market-intelligence/payment-methods-latin-america/.

Ganbold, S. 2021. "E-commerce in the Asia-Pacific Region—Statistics and Facts." https://www.statista.com/topics/7121/e-commerce-in-asia-pacific/#dossierKeyfigures.

Ganti, Akhilesh. 2023. "What Real Gross Domestic Product (Real GDP) Is, How to Calculate It, vs Nominal." Investopedia. https://www.investopedia.com/terms/r/realgdp.asp.

Global Generosity Movement. 2010. "A Handful of Rice." Oxford: Global Generosity Network. Retrieved from the DVD titled "Generosity Resources."

González, Justo. 2002. *Faith and Wealth: A History of Early Christian Ideas on the Origin, Significance and Use of Money*. Eugene, OR: Wipf and Stock.

Green, Nigel. 2017. "Mobile Banking in Asia: The Future Is Now." *AsiaTimes*. (August) https://asiatimes.com/2017/08/mobile-banking-asia-future-now/.

Holcomb, Ronald. 1998. "Harambee! Working Together to Prepare African Missionaries." Dissertation, Western Seminary.

Howarth, Josh. 2023. "Time Spent Using Smartphones (2023 Statistics)." https://explodingtopics.com/blog/smartphone-usage-stats#smartphone-usage-by-region.

IMF. 2022. Projections Table: "Economic Forecasts: Asia and the Pacific." Source: International Monetary Fund World Economic Outlook Database. https://www.imf.org/en/Publications/REO/APAC/Issues/2022/04/25/regional-economic-outlook-for-asia-and-pacific-april-2022.

Jenkins, Philip. 2002. *The Next Christendom: The Coming of Global Christianity*. Oxford: Oxford University Press.

Johnson, Paul. 2014. *More Than Money, More Than Faith: Successfully Raising Missionary Support in the Twenty-First Century*, revised edition. Enumclaw, WA: Pleasant Word.

Johnson, Todd, Gina Zurlo, Albert Hickman, and Peter Crossing. 2017. "Christianity 2018: More African Christians and Counting Martyrs." *International Bulletin of Mission Research* 42 (no. 1). https://journals.sagepub.com/doi/abs/10.1177/2396939317739833.

Kane, Abdoulaye. 2010. *Tontines, caisses de solidarité et banquiers ambulants: Univers des pratiques financières informelles en Afrique.* (Revolving Savings Plans, Solidarity Funds and Itinerant Bankers: The Universe of Informal Financial Practices in Africa). Paris: L'Harmattan.

Keener, Craig. 1993. *The IVP Bible Background Commentary: New Testament.* Downers Grove, IL: InterVarsity Press.

Keller, Tim. 2014. *Every Good Endeavor: Connecting Your Work to God's Work.* New York: Riverhead Books.

Keyes, Lawrence E. 1983. *The Last Age of Missions: A Study of Third World Mission Societies.* Pasadena, CA: William Carey Library.

Kuen, Alfred. 1976. *Parole vivante.* (Living Word New Testament). Braine-l'Alleud, Belgium: Éditeurs de Littérature Biblique.

Kuen, Alfred, Christophe Paya, and Jacques Buchhold. 2005. Study notes, Acts of the Apostles. *Bible d'étude, version Semeur 2000.* (Sowers 2000 Study Bible). Charols, France: Éditions Excelsis.

L. 2014. "How Ethnic Minorities Can Experience Support Raising." *Minister Different—Series: Funding Multiethnic Mission.* http://ministerdifferent.com/can-experience-support-raising/.

Lai, Patrick. 2005. *Tentmaking: The Life and Work of Business as Missions.* Downers Grove, IL: InterVarsity Press.

Le Belzic, Sébastien. 2016. "Les réseaux de la Chinafrique." (The Networks of Chinafrica). *African Business* [French edition] 43: 28–30.

Lederleitner, Mary. 2010. *Cross-Cultural Partnerships: Navigating the Complexities of Money and Mission.* Downers Grove, IL: InterVarsity Press.

Littlefield, Elizabeth. 2014. "Africa: An Investment Opportunity" [Commentary]. *The Baltimore Sun.*

M., Marko. 2022. "29+ Smartphone Usage Statistics: Around the World in 2022." https://leftronic.com/blog/smartphone-usage-statistics/.

MacArthur, John. 2006. Study notes, 1 Corinthians. *La Sainte Bible avec commentaires de John MacArthur.* (The Holy Bible with Commentary by John MacArthur). Geneva, Switzerland: Société biblique de Genève.

Matenga, Jay, and Malcolm Gold. 2016. *Mission in Motion: Speaking Frankly of Mobilization.* Pasadena, CA: William Carey Library.

Maury, Frédéric. 2014. "Épargne en ligne: Tigo propose une version mobile du *susu* traditionnel." (Online Saving: Tigo Proposes a Mobile Version of the Traditional *Susu*). *Jeune Afrique* 37: 15.

McQuilkin, Robertson. 1999. "Stop Spending Money! Breaking the Cycle of Missions Dependency." *Christianity Today* 43, no. 3.

Miniwatts Marketing Group. Internet World Stats: Usage and Population Statistics. 2022. https://internetworldstats.com/stats.htm.

Moon, Steve. 2013. "Missionary Families and Korean Mission Finance: Realities and Concerns." In *Family Accountability in Missions: Korean and Western Case Studies*, edited by Jonathan J. Bonk, 138–48. New Haven, CT: OMSC Publications.

Moravian Church in America. 2018. Denominational website. "A Brief History of the Moravian Church." https://www.moravian.org/2018/07/a-brief-history-of-the-moravian-church/.

Morton, Scott. 2016. *Blindspots: Leading Your Team & Ministry to Full Funding.* Fayetteville, AR: CMM Press.

Morton, Scott. 2017. *Funding Your Ministry: A Field Guide for Raising Personal Support.* 3rd ed. Colorado Springs: NavPress.

Mtata, Kenneth. 2011. *Dignity of Work: Theological and Interdisciplinary Perspectives.* Minneapolis: Lutheran University Press.

Nicole, Jules-Marcel. 1972. *Précis d'Histoire de l'Église.* (Survey of Church History). Nogent-sur-Marne, France: Édition de l'Institut Biblique de Nogent.

O'Connell, Brian. 2020. "History of Alibaba: Timeline and Facts." TheStreet. https://www.thestreet.com/world/history-of-alibaba-15145103.

Ong, Rebecca. 2022. "Remittances to Reach $630 Billion in 2022 with Record Flows into Ukraine." The World Bank. https://www.worldbank.org/en/news/press-release/2022/05/11/remittances-to-reach-630-billion-in-2022-with-record-flows-into-ukraine.

Otaola, Pablo. 2014. "Contextual Support Raising: A Solutions Guest Post." *Minister Different—Series: Funding Multiethnic Mission.* http://ministerdifferent.com/contextual-support-raising/.

Pate, Larry D. 1989. *From Every People: A Handbook of Two-Thirds World Missions with Directory/Histories/Analysis.* Monrovia, CA: MARC.

Perry, Samuel. 2012. "Diversity, Donations, and Disadvantage: The Implications of Personal Fundraising for Racial Diversity in Evangelical Outreach Ministries." *Review of Religious Research* 53, no. 4: 397–418.

Pew Research Center. 2011. "Wealth Gaps Rise to Record Highs Between Whites, Blacks, Hispanics." https://www.pewresearch.org/social-trends/2011/07/26/wealth-gaps-rise-to-record-highs-between-whites-blacks-hispanics/.

RANE–Worldview. 2022. "Security Challenges in Latin America." https://worldview.stratfor.com/topic/security-challenges-latin-america.

Ravitz, Jessica. 2010. "Monks Making Money: A Business Beyond Prayer." CNN. http://www.cnn.com/2010/LIVING/05/27/monks.money/.

Reuters. 2022. "JPMorgan Cuts U.S. GDP Estimates for 2022 and 2023." https://www.reuters.com/markets/us/jpmorgan-cuts-us-gdp-estimates-2022-2023-2022-05-18/.

Robinson, Eric. 2014a. "How Support Raising Keeps Parachurch Ministries White." *Minister Different—Series: Funding Multiethnic Mission.* (February) http://ministerdifferent.com/support-raising-white/.

Robinson, Eric. 2014b. "Support Raising Is Not as Biblically Based as We Think It Is." *Minister Different—Series: Funding Multiethnic Mission.* (February) http://ministerdifferent.com/not-as-biblically-based/.

Robinson, Eric. 2014c. "Unsent Peoples: How Fixing Support Raising Could Help Fulfill the Great Commission." *Minister Different—Series: Funding Multiethnic Mission.* (March) http://ministerdifferent.com/unsent-peoples/.

Robinson, Eric. 2014d. "Turning the White Ship Parachurch Around?"—A Solutions Guest Post, by Scott Bessenecker. *Minister Different—Series: Funding Multiethnic Mission.* (April) http://ministerdifferent.com/unsent-peoples/turning-parachurch-ship-around/.

Romero, Teresa. 2022. "Gross Domestic Product (GDP) Real Growth Rate in Latin America and the Caribbean in 2021 and 2022, by Country." statista.com/statistics/1032072/gross-domestic-product-growth-latin-america-caribbean-country/.

Sembène, Elimane. 2015. "Crowdfunding: une aubaine pour les start-up africaines" (Crowdfunding: A Windfall for African Start-ups). *African Business Journal* 16: 42–61. Dakar, Senegal: Afrique Challenge.

SLA (She Leads Africa). 2022. "Five Top E-commerce Platforms in Africa." https://sheleadsafrica.org/growth-of-ecommerce/.

Smith, Glenn. 2005. "La mission de Dieu dans le monde urbain du XXIe siècle." (The Mission of God in the Urban World of the 21st Century). *Œcuménisme* (March/June): 157–58, 46–52.

Smith, Glenn. 2009. "La mission de Dieu et la vocation évolutive de l'Église au Québec." (The Mission of God and the Evolving Vocation of the Church in Quebec). *L'Évangile et le monde urbanisé.* Montreal: Direction Chrétienne, Section 1: article 8.

Smith, Glenn. 2017. *Thinking After … Acting Again.* Montreal: Christian Direction.

Songhai Advisory LL (n.d.). "Country Risk." *Invest in Africa.* https://www.investinafrica.com/Uploads//contentuploads/98123d72-c1f7-4662-a2ce-2de7819d8384/file.pdf.

Statista. 2022a. "Direct Investment Position of the United States in Africa from 2000 to 2021." https://www.statista.com/statistics/188594/united-states-direct-investments-in-africa-since-2000/.

Statista. 2022b. "Number of E-commerce Users in Asia from 2017 to 2025." https://www.statista.com/forecasts/1259097/e-commerce-users-asia.

Steffen, Tom, and Mike Barnett, eds. 2006. *Business as Mission: From Impoverished to Empowered.* Pasadena, CA: William Carey Library.

Stevens, R. Paul. 1999. *The Other Six Days: Vocation, Work, and Ministry in Biblical Perspective.* Vancouver, Canada: Regent College Publishing.

Swanson, Eric. 2010. "Nine Game-Changers for Global Missions." *Leadership Network.* https://ministryformation.com.au/attachments/article/227/Nine_Game_Changers.pdf.

Sy, Mohamadou. 2013. "Le renouveau de l'Afrique." (The Revival of Africa). *African Business Journal* 5: 32–43.

Taylor, William. 1994. *Kingdom Partnerships for Synergy in Missions*. Pasadena, CA: William Carey Library.

Tennent, Timothy. 2010. *Invitation to World Missions: A Trinitarian Missiology for the Twenty-First Century*. Grand Rapids: Kregel Publications.

Tonby, Oliver, Jonathan Woetzel, Noshir Kaka, Wonsik Choi, Anand Swaminathan, Jeongmin Seong, Brant Carson, Lily Ma. 2020. "How Asia Can Boost Growth through Technological Leapfrogging." McKinsey.com. Discussion paper. https://www.mckinsey.com/featured-insights/asia-pacific/how-asia-can-boost-growth-through-technological-leapfrogging.

Traveling Team, The. (n.d.) *About Missions*. http://www.aboutmissions.org/statistics.html.

Trebilco, Paul. 2010. "Prosélyte." *Le Grand Dictionnaire de la Bible*. (The Large Bible Dictionary). Charols, France: Excelsis.

Trites, Allison. 2015. Study notes, Acts of the Apostles. *NLT Illustrated Study Bible*. Carol Stream, IL: Tyndale House Publishers.

Umar, Khalid. 2021. "1.7 Billion People Don't Have a Bank Account—But Mobile Banking Could Change Their Lives." BrinkNews.com. https://www.brinknews.com/bridging-the-digital-divide-to-widen-financial-services-in-central-asia/.

UN-ECLAC. 2022. "Net Foreign Direct Investment" chart. United Nations Economic Commission for Latin America and the Caribbean. https://statistics.cepal.org/portal/cepalstat/dashboard.html?indicator_id=1824&area_id=454&lang=en.

UN-ESCAP. 2021. "Foreign Direct Investment Trends and Outlook in Asia and the Pacific 2021/2022." United Nations Economic and Social Commission for Asia and the Pacific. https://unescap.org/kp/2021/foreign-direct-investment-trends-and-outlook-asia-and-pacific-20212022.

UNCTAD. 2022. "Investment Flows to Africa Reached a Record $83 Billion in 2021." United Nations Conference on Trade and Development. https://unctad.org/news/investment-flows-africa-reached-record-83-billion-2021.

Ventura, Luca. 2022. "Richest Countries in the World 2022." *Global Finance*. https://www.gfmag.com/global-data/economic-data/richest-countries-in-the-world.

Verwer, George. 2000. *Out of the Comfort Zone: A Compelling Vision for Transforming Global Mission*. Bloomington, MN: Bethany House.

Walls, Andrew. 1996. *The Missionary Movement in Christian History: Studies in the Transformation of the Faith*. Maryknoll, NY: Orbis Books.

Welch, Tim. 2019. *Analyse et propositions de financement missionnaire dans les églises évangéliques du Monde majoritaire*. (Analysis and Proposals for Mission Funding in Evangelical Churches in the Majority World). Dissertation, Abidjan, Côte d'Ivoire: Université de l'Alliance Chrétienne d'Abidjan.

Wilson, Fred. 1994. "A New Paradigm for Cross-Cultural Missions." Dissertation, Western Conservative Baptist Seminary.

Wong, James. 1973. *Missions from the Third World: A World Survey of Non-Western Missions in Asia, Africa and Latin America.* Singapore: Church Growth Study Center.

World Bank. 2022a. "MENA Economic Update: Reality Check: Forecasting Growth in the Middle East and North Africa in Times of Uncertainty." https://www. worldbank.org/en/region/mena/publication/mena-economic-update-forecasting-growth-in-the-middle-east-and-north-africa-in-times-of-uncertainty.

World Bank. 2022b. "Global Economic Prospects: Europe and Central Asia." https://www.worldbank.org/en/region/eca/brief/global-economic-prospects-europe-and-central-asia.

World Bank. 2022c. "The World Bank in Africa." https://www.worldbank.org/en/region/afr/overview.

Yamamori, Tetsunao, and Kenneth A. Eldred, eds. 2003. *On Kingdom Business: Transforming Missions Through Entrepreneurial Strategies.* Wheaton: Crossway Books.

You also might be interested in—

The Realities of Money & Missions: Global Challenges & Case Studies

Jonathan J. Bonk, Michel G. Distefano, J. Nelson Jennings, Jinbong Kim, and Jae Hoon Lee, editors | 290-page Paperback & ePub

---

Integrity, Viability, and Accountability

Perhaps there is no greater challenge in missions than money. Paul reminds us, "For we are taking pains to do what is right, not only in the eyes of the Lord but also in the eyes of man" (2 Cor 8:21).

Money sufficient to assure the viability of one's life work carries with it an insidious ethical virus that can easily infect the integrity and accountability of its stewards. *The Realities of Money & Missions* provides a unique level of credibility and transparency as it calls for evangelicals to reevaluate their relationship with money, both personally and corporately. Global case studies, workshops, and testimonials cover a broad range of topics such as:

- Misalignment between fiscal theology and practice

- Environmental stewardship, community development, and business as mission

- Mobilization, fundraising practices, and "faith financing"

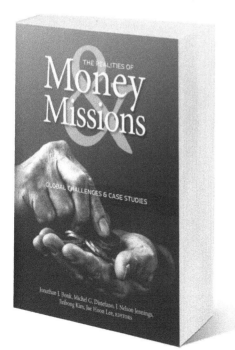

- Short-term missions, patronage, and dependency

- Power dynamics and structural injustice

The Realities of Money & Missions was not written by experts in the fields of investment, money management, or fundraising, but by men and women whose calling as missionaries, pastors, and administrators has brought them face-to-face with the complex, real-life issues involving the intersection of money and ministry. Read on and be challenged to change.

WILLIAM CAREY
PUBLISHING
visit us at missionbooks.org

CPSIA information can be obtained
at www.ICGtesting.com
Printed in the USA
LVHW031250030523
745890LV00011B/903